NEW · MASTERS *of the*
WOODEN BOX

EXPANDING THE BOUNDARIES OF BOX MAKING

NEW·MASTERS *of the* WOODEN BOX

EXPANDING THE BOUNDARIES OF BOX MAKING

OSCAR P. FITZGERALD

Published with the exhibition "Boxes and Their Makers," Fall 2009,
Messler Gallery of the Center for Furniture Craftsmanship, Rockport, Maine.

FOX CHAPEL
PUBLISHING

© 2009 by Fox Chapel Publishing Company, Inc.

New Masters of the Wooden Box is an original work, first published in 2009 by Fox Chapel Publishing Company, Inc.

ISBN 978-1-56523-392-8

Publisher's Cataloging-in-Publication Data

Fitzgerald, Oscar P.

   New masters of the wooden box : expanding the boundaries of box
   making / by Oscar Fitzgerald. -- East Petersburg, PA : Fox
   Chapel Publishing, c2009

        p. ; cm.

        ISBN: 978-1-56523-392-8

        Includes index.

        1. Wooden boxes. 2. Painted wooden boxes. 3. Ornamental
   boxes. 4. Woodworkers--Biography. I. Title.

TT200 .F58 2009
684/.08--dc22   2009

To learn more about the other great books from Fox Chapel Publishing, or to find a retailer near you, call toll-free 800-457-9112 or visit us at *www.FoxChapelPublishing.com*.

Note to Authors: We are always looking for talented authors to write new books in our area of woodworking, design, and related crafts. Please send a brief letter describing your idea to Acquisition Editor, 1970 Broad Street, East Petersburg, PA 17520.

Printed in China
First printing: August 2009

ABOUT THE AUTHOR

Oscar P. Fitzgerald, Ph.D., earned his master and doctorate degrees in history from Georgetown University. He served as director of the Navy Museum in Washington, D.C., and curator for Tingey House, the oldest residence in the Navy, until he decided to pursue fulltime his passion as a furniture historian and decorative arts consultant.

Fitzgerald's consulting includes work for Dumbarton House, the headquarters for The National Society of The Colonial Dames of America; Arlington House, the Robert E. Lee Memorial; and the Clara Barton National Historic Site. He is a member of the faculty of the Smithsonian Institution/Corcoran School Master's Program in the History of Decorative Arts, where he teaches all of the courses on the history of American furniture and the contemporary studio furniture movement.

Among Fitzgerald's many publications is *Four Centuries of American Furniture*, the standard reference work in the field. In 2004, he was awarded a prestigious James Renwick Research Fellowship that funded research for a seminal essay on the studio furniture field that appeared in the 2005 issue of *Furniture Studio*. His most recent book, *Studio Furniture of the Renwick Gallery*, was published in 2008. A longtime student and collector of eighteenth and nineteenth century American furniture, he has also amassed an extensive collection of antique and contemporary boxes.

ABOUT THE OTHER JURORS

Toni Sikes is founder, artistic advisor, board member, and former chief executive officer of The Guild, a publishing company dedicated to helping artists market and sell their work through printed sourcebooks and The Artful Home Website and catalog. Sikes is also the author of *The Artful Home: Using Art & Craft to Create Living Spaces You'll Love* and writes a weekly blog, The Artful Life (blog.guild.com). She is on the boards of the Craft Emergency Relief Fund, Aid to Artisans, The Greater Madison Chamber of Commerce, and The Wisconsin Technology Council. Sikes currently serves as a senior advisor at Gruppo, Levey & Co., a New York investment bank, where she leads an initiative to help young technology companies in their financing and M&A strategies.

Kevin Wallace is director of the Beatrice Wood Center for the Arts in Ojai, California. For more than a decade, he has worked as an independent curator and writer, focusing on contemporary art in craft media. He is on the board of directors of Collectors of Wood Art and serves on the advisory board of the Handweavers Guild of America. He is a contributing editor for *American Woodturner* and *Shuttle, Spindle, and Dyepot*, and a regular contributor to Crafts Art International (Australia) and *Woodturning* magazine (England). Wallace is the author or co-author of eight books, including *New Masters of Woodturning* from Fox Chapel Publishing.

ABOUT THE CURATOR

Peter Korn is executive director of the Center for Furniture Craftsmanship, a nonprofit woodworking school in Rockport, Maine, which he founded in 1992. He is also chief curator of the center's Messler Gallery, from which the traveling exhibition *Boxes and Their Makers* originated. A furniture maker since 1974, Korn is the author of *Woodworking Basics: Mastering the Essentials of Craftsmanship* (Taunton Press, 2003) and *The Woodworker's Guide to Hand Tools* (Taunton Press, 1998.)

FOREWORD

by Peter Korn

As Oscar Fitzgerald's introduction (page 11) illustrates, boxes have a pedigree as ancient as civilization itself. The sheer variety of human invention they record is astounding. Yet, for all of that, the contemporary boxes within these pages represent something new under the sun. Why they are novel, and what they tell us about ourselves, is well worth exploring.

Full Term by Ray Jones.

Every historical box to which Fitzgerald refers—no matter how ornate or plain, precious or practical, decorative or useful, highly crafted or rustic—was created to fill a functional niche in a social environment. Hatboxes, snuff boxes, Bible boxes, and candle boxes may seem quaint today, but the craftsmen who made them were addressing practical needs imposed by the customs of their times.

The boxes featured within these pages are fundamentally different. They may variously be described as playful, elegant, beautiful, whimsical, sculptural, functional, conceptual, precious, obsessive…but they are not defined by intended use. Where earlier boxes were made to serve, these boxes are made as vehicles for self-expression. Their ultimate use is left to the whims of their purchasers. As the interviews within this book indicate, the makers of these boxes didn't go into their workshops because there was a shortage of containers in the world. Rather, they went into their workshops on voyages of creative exploration to transform raw materials into expressive objects.

Considered in the long view, this new breed of box maker originated at the convergence of two tectonic shifts in Western consciousness. The first began approximately 250 years ago with the Industrial Revolution, which gradually destroyed the economic foundation for practicing what we now call craft as a trade. Prior to the Industrial Revolution, virtually every manmade object had been the product of individual human agency and skill. Subsequent to it, making things "by hand" became a potentially revolutionary act itself— something one did in opposition to prevailing cultural norms.

At the same time that craft was being displaced, the way in which people thought of themselves as individuals took a radical turn. For all of recorded history, beliefs about the nature of humanity and the purposes of life had been in flux. But every belief system had agreed that a person became fully human only through participation in a larger entity—whether that entity was a tribe, a polity, a divine order, or a social class. By the mid-twentieth century, however, the dominant model of the individual had become a fully autonomous internal self. Where people had once looked to external sources such as society, God, and nature for validation, truth was now to be found within. With this change, external scaffoldings fell away, and the task of constructing one's identity became the life project of the individual.

It was in this cultural setting, starting in the 1940s, that craft found new relevance as an alternative lifestyle. Craft offered a model of adulthood in which creative, self-expressive work promised to be a wellspring

---

This was the birth of the Studio Craft movement, and it is the cultural framework within which the makers featured here practice their craft today.

---

of identity and meaning. The post-industrial craftsman worked at an occupation that had no socioeconomic rationale and therefore no prescribed mores. He could invent himself from the ground up through the genius of his own two hands. This was the birth of the Studio Craft movement, and it is the cultural framework within which the makers featured here practice their craft today.

How then, to read the boxes presented within these pages? There is a contemporary notion that the artist has greater access to his inner truth than the rest of us have to ours. In her book, *Thinking With Things*, author Esther Pasztory says:

> By the mid-twentieth century the concept of the shaman had been transformed into a metaphor for the artist; the artist is now identified as someone on the edge of madness who can ascend or descend into realms of unconsciousness unavailable to others and bring back gifts for the community in the form of works of art.[1]

While not everyone would consider the makers of these boxes to be shamans at the edge of madness, there is no doubt that in constructing their own narratives of identity they reach beyond socially sanctioned modules to the raw source of experience. Each time they engage creatively in the effort to bring something new and meaningful into the world, they are thinking with the language of material, form, and technique to invent new ways of being in the world. In this context, each box is the summation of a discussion, a repository of questions asked and answers found. Ultimately, what it was made to contain is a lively point of view as to what it is to be human and how one might live in these times.

[1] Pasztory, Esther. *Thinking With Things*.
University of Texas Press, 2005, page 93.

CONTENTS

COVER

Moue, Box No. 1147
by Peter Lloyd.

TITLE PAGE

Inner Eye Box by Bonnie
Bishoff and J. M. Syron.

OPPOSITE

Multi-Axis Box V by
Andrew Potocnik.

INTRODUCTION

Boxes through the Ages

Greek mythology tells us Pandora's box contained all of the sins and evils of the world. The gods warned her not to open the box but when her curiosity got the better of her, she raised the lid and scattered disease and trouble all over the world. By the time she could shut the lid, only hope remained. Who can resist opening a box?

What is a Box?

Boxes are among the most ancient of humankind's works. Usually with four sides, a bottom, and a lid, boxes contain everything imaginable. Lids can be either hinged to the case or detachable, and secured with a hasp or lock to protect the contents. The box can be square, round, oblong, or oval, though in eighteenth century France, craftsmen fashioned them in many unlikely shapes such as satchels, tricorn hats, wine casks, and sedan chairs. Although typically made of wood, some boxes in the eighteenth century were fashioned of shells, fossils, and petrified wood. Silver and gold ones also were made, many embellished with enameled decoration or encrusted with precious stones.

Some boxes have no lid at all and others had no sides. Alarm boxes, compass boxes, and gearboxes, for example, were designed to encase fragile equipment, and baseball boxes were merely the place where the pitcher, umpire, batter, or coaches could stand. Boxes marked off on a printed page separate sidebars from the main text.

Boxes by definition contain something. They can be as large as a big-box store or small enough to hold cuff links or a tiny ring. Some were designed to contain people gathered together for specific activities—theater, jury, press, or sentry boxes. Metaphorical boxes are made up of constraints real or imagined. If you are in a box or have been boxed in, you have a problem that has no easy escape. Black boxes contain the unknowable.

The idea of a box is so familiar that *Webster's Unabridged Dictionary* lists nearly fifty objects with attributes of a box. These include tools like box wrenches, seating like box pews, animals like box crabs, sewing items like box pleats, vehicles like box cars, clothing like box coats, architectural elements like box locks, topographical features like box canyons, and techniques like boxlike football defenses and artillery barrages.

Ancient Boxes

Chests and boxes were among the oldest of domestic objects. Distinguished from chests by their smaller size, boxes have been made at least since the time of the pharaohs

A small cosmetics case with two ointment vessels constructed from wood and faience, Egypt, circa 1400 B.C.E. The piece is on display at the Museum Berlin.

Numerous square boxes had flat tops or gabled lids, often of ebony and cedar with ivory inlay. A rectangular wooden box with a hunchbacked lid was decorated with scenes of the hunt or of battles painted on ivory panels on the top, and with floral and animal depictions on the sides. It probably held the king's robes. Like most of the wooden boxes found in the tomb, it was made with mortise-and-tenon joints and carefully cut dovetails—the same joints used by woodworkers today. The box was secured by string threaded around mushroom-shaped knobs and tied with a knot that was then sealed.

In addition to the rectangular, lidded boxes, a nineteen-inch-high wooden box with doors probably held a statue of the king and his queen. The surface was covered with sheets of embossed gold, perhaps depicting the king's coronation. A small, double box still held a brown unguent with spoons, should the pharaoh need to take his medicine. Another box cut out of a solid piece of wood only two inches high held a miniature carving of the king lying on a bier supported by two lions. The superintendent of building works in the Necropolis, who ironically may have been the man who revealed the tomb's location to subsequent grave robbers, had placed it in the tomb.

Although most of the boxes were made of reed that grew abundantly in the Nile River, or wood covered with gold or ivory, some were fashioned from alabaster. One box carved from a solid piece of alabaster contained four canopic jars that held the pharaoh's vital organs.

in ancient Egypt. The numerous boxes recovered from King Tutankhamen's tomb were typical of those that held everyday items the pharaohs would need in the afterlife. Most were rectangular, but one for a mirror was shaped like an ankh, the hieroglyph for life. Curved ones held bows or ceremonial hats. One small box held the mummified bodies of two stillborn babies that may have been the king's children. Four rectangular boxes with inlaid ivory and ebony checkerboard tops came with markers for games similar to modern-day chess or checkers.

Since ancient Egyptian times, boxes were found throughout the world, both in the West and in the Orient. They have survived from the Nubians who were the bitter rivals of the Egyptians in North Africa, from the Sumerian kingdom at Ur, and from the Assyrian Empire in the Middle East. They have also been found in the Indus Valley of India and in Minoan and Mycenaean cultures of the Mediterranean. Box making thrived and was transmitted to the Roman Empire by the Greeks. Many Greek boxes were made of clay. The Romans favored small silver and ivory boxes for perfume and cosmetics. They used larger boxes for food storage.

After the fall of the Roman Empire, boxes survived in monasteries and castles in Europe during the Middle Ages. Many held vestments, holy relics, incense, and plate. Small caskets or decorated boxes served as jewel or valuables boxes. Larger cast-iron boxes were common, and medieval dispatch boxes typically had two keys, one each for sender and recipient.

Work Boxes

Most boxes that survived during the Middle Ages were utilitarian and rather plain. During the Renaissance, however, elegant box making was revived. For example, at the end of the sixteenth century Queen Elizabeth I owned a pearl-covered box where she kept her bracelets and other jewelry, and another carved, gilded and painted one held her silver combs, perfume bottles, and a mirror. Boxes for storing sewing supplies, dressing boxes for personal make-up items, and desk boxes for writing equipment and

important documents were among the most elaborate boxes.

By the seventeenth century, a box maker's guild had been incorporated in England, and its members specialized in wooden boxes with compartments and drawers and slanting lids to hold books for reading. They were decorated with chip carving, applied split spindles, and bosses. Other seventeenth century boxes were fitted with locks and covered with incised leather. Serving as the portable desks of the time, these boxes held valuable books (but few Bibles, even though they are called Bible boxes), writing equipment, and papers. In the eighteenth century, as papers and accounts proliferated and boxes grew larger, they were placed

ABOVE

Larger than either a trinket box or a letter box, this early nineteenth century skin-covered document box is trimmed with leather strips.

RIGHT

English tortoise shell needle case in the shape of an early nineteenth century knife box with gold and silver trim.

pincushions. Shallow ones that anticipated the popular bandboxes of the nineteenth century held gloves and lace.

Equally complex were boxes covered in intricate straw-work. Apparently of Near Eastern origin, the technique was particularly popular in Continental Europe by the mid-seventeenth century, and was introduced into England by French prisoners of war. Tiny strips of straw were split with special tools, colored, and then glued onto a backing paper to form geometric designs or still life and landscape views. The paper was then glued to various kinds of boxes and was even applied to furniture.

In England, as in America in the eighteenth century, most genteel young women were taught to sew. They owned boxes of richly figured wood or with japanned decoration to carry pincushions, spools of thread, picks, punches, bobbins, thimbles, crochet hooks, needle cases, and scissors. The women themselves painted some. In the 1830s, tiered spool boxes became popular. They were surmounted by a pincushion and fitted with eyelets through which thread could be pulled. At the same time the Shakers sold special "carriers," round or oval containers with handles that were lined with silk and filled with pin cushions, needle cases, emery bags, and wax.

Workboxes for women continued in popularity throughout the eighteenth and early nineteenth century. By 1800, many were attached to stands, but portable ones were still common. In his *The Cabinet-Maker and Upholsterer's Drawing-Book* (1792), Thomas Sheraton illustrated a square

on stands, and the modern desk was born. Still, the portable lap desk continued in popularity well into the nineteenth century.

Both men and women used dressing boxes in the seventeenth and eighteenth centuries. Ones for men contained razors, strops and hones, scissors, penknives, and a looking glass. Many were imported to America from England, and others with japanned decoration were made in the Orient. By the mid-eighteenth century, dressing glasses that sat on tables replaced the portable boxes.

The reign of the Stuarts in seventeenth century England saw the popularity of elaborate needlework-covered boxes with hipped tops. Ladies used them as dressing or toilet boxes to hold perfume, cosmetics, and mirrors, or as writing boxes to contain paper, ink, and sand. Others served as sewing boxes complete with needle cases and

"Lady's Traveling Box" fitted up for writing, dressing, and sewing equipment. It contained compartments for ink and an adjustable writing surface covered with green cloth; a place for scissors and powder, pomatum, and perfume bottles; and a removable dressing glass. There was even a space to store rings and a clever little windlass for rolling up lace as it was worked.

As early as the seventeenth century, cabinetmakers made miniature chests of drawers to match the prevailing furniture style. The chest served as a box for the drawers and each drawer was a box unto itself. Miniature English oak chests with drawers have survived from each of the style periods of the eighteenth century—William and Mary, Queen Anne, Chippendale, and Federal.

By the early nineteenth century the miniature chest became increasingly common, and they were made in abundance in the Empire style. By the mid-nineteenth century, with the introduction of factory-made, Victorian furniture, the miniature chest grew more rare, but ones made by amateur cabinetmakers turned up well into the twentieth century. Among the most interesting are tramp art boxes, fashioned from wood salvaged from cigar boxes or crates, and decorated with elaborate chip carving.

As early as 1800, the manufacture of wooden boxes began to be threatened as sheet tin was imported in quantity from England. Sheets of iron coated with tin were durable and easily fashioned into boxes. Tin boxes were made with either flat or domed tops, often japanned and decorated

This dressing box, fitted for makeup containers, was made about 1840 in Baltimore, Maryland. Traces of the original gilt shells and flowers decorate the sides. The underside of the lid probably held a mirror.

with flowers. Toleware (fancy tinware) was decorated by stenciling or hand painting. The background was usually black or red, decorated with fruits, flowers, and naturalistic designs. Tin boxes gradually supplanted the wooden desk box to hold papers and documents and other valuables, including cash.

Snuff and Tobacco Boxes

The heyday for English boxes was in the eighteenth century, and often the most extravagant work was lavished on the tiny snuffbox. After the discovery of tobacco in the New World in the seventeenth century, the elaborate ritual of inhaling powdered tobacco spread throughout Europe. Many gentlemen owned multiple boxes to match their various degrees of dress and

Images courtesy Sallea Antiques.

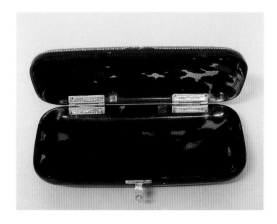

the formality of the occasion. Madame de Pompadour, mistress of Louis XV, reputedly had a different snuffbox for every day of the year.

Most snuffboxes were oval or oblong, but some were round or more rarely triangular. They also came in the shape of birds, human heads, and animals. The cheapest were made of potato pulp while jewelers or goldsmiths, who decorated them with gold, enamel, and diamonds, created the most expensive cases. Tortoise shell was particularly popular, followed by mother-of-pearl and silver. A few snuffboxes were carved out of solid agate and covered with openwork silver. Some of the best were painted enamel boxes from Battersea, England, or produced in porcelain in Chelsea. Themes included sporting events, country scenes, gardens, and flowers. Lids were further enhanced with portraits of classical figures or copies of Old Masters.

By the nineteenth century, the custom of taking snuff declined, and cigarette and cigar smoking increased. As elegant snuffboxes fell out of fashion, they were replaced with larger cigarette and cigar cases. Early in the nineteenth century, most tobacco boxes were turned out of pewter, brass, or copper, while cheaper ones came in pinchbeck, an alloy of zinc and copper that simulated gold. A particularly interesting variant was produced in Lancashire, England, early in the century when watchmaking became mechanized and the watchmakers turned to making elaborate, locked tobacco boxes with clock faces. Wooden boxes were inexpensive to make, and by the late-nineteenth century the familiar, six-board cigar box was common. Cigarette and cigar boxes survived well into the twentieth century, though now they are mostly of cardboard.

As tobacco smoking spread, matchboxes to light the weed proliferated. By the nineteenth century, they were often made in the likenesses of famous people such as Queen Victoria, Chancellor Bismarck of Germany, and Christopher Columbus. Others took odd shapes of basketballs, dominos, and violins. Vesta boxes, holding short wooden matches named for the Roman goddess of the hearth, were typically shaped like small books.

Gift and Souvenir Boxes

As a measure of their preciousness, snuffboxes were often given as gifts or to celebrate heroic deeds or special events. Boxes were issued to commemorate the

hot-air balloon assent of the Montgolfier brothers in the late-eighteenth century and to celebrate the victory of Admiral Vernon over the Spanish at Portobello in 1739. Many were awarded to the Duke of Wellington for his victory over Napoleon at the Battle of Waterloo.

Since the eighteenth century, visitors to Tunbridge Wells, a spa in Kent, England, could buy souvenir boxes inlaid with intricate mosaics cut from tiny rods of wood. The decoration was originally abstract, but soon the boxes exhibited portraits of well-known celebrities or views of the spa itself. By the mid-nineteenth century, they featured depictions of cathedrals, castles, and country estates.

Political leaders and ambassadors exchanged snuffboxes to commemorate diplomacy and treaty signings. Charles II presented numerous sumptuous boxes containing jewels or spices to foreign diplomats during his reign in the mid-seventeenth century. Many were decorated with elaborate veneer cut in the oyster pattern, or with marquetry designs of birds and butterflies, acanthus leaves, flowers, and arabesques. A box did not always have to be

given to facilitate negotiations. According to Talleyrand, the early nineteenth century French statesman, offering snuff during diplomatic negotiations provided a convenient excuse to stop and think.

Some richly decorated snuffboxes were presented as gifts to friends or lovers, or out of gratitude as a form of payment. Recipients could sell a gold box for money. George IV commissioned snuffboxes to give as gifts to foreign ambassadors attending his coronation in 1821. In the early 1830s, Captain Isaac Hull, the commandant of the Washington Navy Yard and a hero of the War of 1812, gave a small, turned snuffbox to Congressman Henry Wise. Wise served on the House Naval Affairs Committee.

ABOVE

Tunbridge ware nesting boxes made as souvenirs from the Tunbridge Wells spa in Kent, England. The geometrical mosaics on these boxes gave way to pictorial decoration by the nineteenth century.

LEFT

This box is made of cloves strung on bamboo string and sewn together around a wire frame. It is a traditional craft practiced in the spice region of Bali in Indonesia. Now sold as tourist souvenirs, the boxes were once presented as gifts to elders or used for storing medicinal items.

ABOVE

American apple wood jewelry or valuable box dated 1825 with a unique locking system. Strips of wood fitted with blocks slide in rabbets cut into the interior surfaces of each side of the box. When the strips are pushed down, the blocks engage notches cut into the top edge of each drawer.

Sailors who made scrimshaw ditty boxes and other items for their loved ones at home continued the tradition of gift boxes into the nineteenth century. In Germany, and also in Pennsylvania, where so many of their countrymen immigrated during the eighteenth century, brides would be given painted oval or round boxes decorated with flowers and figures as a traditional wedding present containing trinkets and ribbons.

Boxing Day, falling the day after Christmas, is celebrated in Britain, Canada, and several other countries, as a day to give gift boxes to servants and trades people. Although the exact origin of the custom is obscure, it may relate to the practice of opening church poor-boxes at Christmas time, or to the fact that servants had to work on Christmas Day and were rewarded the day after with gifts—much like today's Christmas bonus.

Personal Boxes

In addition to gift boxes, a number of other specialized containers were popular in the eighteenth and nineteenth centuries. Gentlemen carried nutmeg and graters to flavor their custard, and had pillboxes in their pockets. Different boxes held breath mints and candy, often in elegant boot-shaped boxes and other forms. Comfit boxes filled with candied fruit or seeds were also

popular during the nineteenth century, and at the coronation of Edward VII in 1902, they were even sold as souvenirs of the celebration.

In the eighteenth century, women carried round, oval or heart-shaped patch boxes to store swatches of silk or taffeta that they applied to their faces to hide the ravages of smallpox and other blemishes. Fancy boxes of silver, gold, ivory, or enamel were often fitted with a gum-pot and brush to stick the fabric patch to the cheek. Other boxes, similar to women's compacts today, held mirrors, rouge, and kohl for the eyes.

In an age when open sewers flowed in the streets and horse manure was everywhere, the *vinaigrette*—often disguised as a watch, book, purse, egg, or other everyday item—contained perfumed sponges or smelling salts that could be sniffed to blot out unpleasant odors. The *vinaigrette* recalled the earlier tradition of carrying a perforated box containing a ball of aromatic spices, called a pomander, to ward off infections.

A small box called an *etui* completed the ensemble of the well-dressed woman. Since the early seventeenth century, these small boxes, much like modern-day purses, were suspended from a women's *chatelaine*, or hook, that might also carry a watch or a bunch of keys. An *etui* contained all manner of personal items such as paper, knives, pencils, tweezers, scissors, spoons and forks, penknives to sharpen quill pens, perfume, pins, corkscrews, toothpicks, and on occasion, compasses. It was not unlike a French *necessaire*, which contained similar items, or the Japanese *inro*, a box that hung from the *netsuke* toggle attached to a cord tied around the waist.

Among the ubiquitous containers are jewelry boxes, usually fitted with satin or velvet and divided into compartments to hold expensive body adornments. By the mid-eighteenth century, trinket boxes to hold less-expensive items became popular. Trinkets were essentially small ornaments including jewelry, but also chains, beads,

buckles, ribbons, and pendants. The women at female academies that sprung up around the United States in the early nineteenth century decorated many of these square or octagonal boxes. These trinket boxes and jewelry boxes continue in popularity to this day.

Boxes for Clothes

Most clothing was folded and stored in boxes or chests, not hung in closets, until well into the nineteenth century. Hats required their own special boxes, and some boxes accommodated wigs as well. Since the seventeenth century, special boxes protected hats fashioned of costly beaver pelts. Tricorn hats made of felt required triangular boxes usually of cardboard lined with newspaper. By the early nineteenth century, the tricorn was superseded by felt top hats with high crowns and narrow brims. The height of the crown and the width of the brim varied from year to year, much like the width of modern-day ties. Women, who seldom went bare-headed in the eighteenth or nineteenth centuries, stored their bonnets in special boxes too, along with their stylish ivory, horn, or tortoiseshell combs.

Special oval or round pasteboard boxes were designed both for storage and for travel. As early as 1598, a treatise on the duties of serving men in England indicated that they were expected to accompany the ladies with boxes containing their "ruffles and other accessories." These were the precursors of the popular bandboxes of the first half of the nineteenth century. They carried removable cuffs and collars (neck bands), and all sorts of women's bagatelles. Bigger ones held dresses, and smaller ones contained jewelry, gloves, lace, ribbons, and beads.

Usually made by commercial box makers or wallpaper manufacturers, the pasteboard boxes were lined with newspaper and covered with printed or stenciled paper or wallpaper. Some were sold in graduated sizes for convenient storage when not in use. Many were decorated with images of public places like the New York City Hall or commemorated historic events like hot-air balloon ascents or the opening of the Erie Canal. Others featured classical subjects, floral patterns, or sailing ships.

Although some of the cardboard boxes came with cotton bags to protect them, the most durable boxes were fabricated out of wood. The best-known maker of wooden boxes was Hannah Davis in New Hampshire. She fashioned the sides of her boxes of thin slices of spruce, cut pine for the bottoms and top, and then covered the exterior with printed paper. Used mostly as trunks during travel, bandboxes fell out of favor as trains and steamboats replaced coach travel. For that, durable, leather-covered, wooden trunks decorated with brass tacks were necessary.

Boxes in the Kitchen

During the eighteenth century, several specialized types of box evolved for the storage of tea, spirits, and dining utensils. Bottle cases held glass containers filled with various spirits. Some also were fitted with racks for wine glasses. With the introduction of tea drinking into England by Catherine of Braganza, the Portuguese wife of Charles II in the seventeenth century, tea caddies proliferated. (A "caddy" was originally a measure of weight, but it soon became

associated with the container for tea.) Usually with two compartments, these little boxes held both black and green tea. Boxes to house knives and spoons developed late in the eighteenth century to sit on newly popular sideboards. Robert Adam and his competitors designed elegant vase-shaped ones made of rich mahogany, while others were fitted with sloping lids to cover tiers of eating utensils. Open boxes with a center divider that also served as a handle performed the same storage function throughout the nineteenth and twentieth centuries but in a much less elegant manner.

Since colonial times, salt was used primarily as a preservative, but also for seasoning. Saltboxes with slanted lids typically hung on the wall near the hearth to keep the salt dry. Most were wood and, at least in Pennsylvania, were usually painted with tulips, floral decorations, or geometric motifs. Although a few porcelain boxes were imported from China, brass, copper, and bell-metal ones were more common.

Throughout the seventeenth and eighteenth centuries, tinder and candle boxes also hung near the fireplace. By the

RIGHT TOP

A nineteenth century, American treenware storage box carved from a solid block of walnut.

RIGHT BOTTOM

Circa 1800 filigree work (paper wrapped around a quill) hexagonal tea caddy embellished with a shield-shaped ivory escutcheon and a mother-of-pearl medallion carved in China.

or oval boxes up to two feet in diameter mostly purchased from local woodworkers. Rectangular ones, often on a stand, held bread dough. Large ones held butter, cheese, and herbs. Smaller ones contained sugar and meal. The smallest were for spices. The Shakers made the best ones. They steam-bent ash or maple strips around molds, secured the strips with copper rivets, added pine bottoms and tops, and then painted or varnished the entire assembly. By the mid-nineteenth century, boxes manufactured in factories were available in sets or nests. Larger boxes that held seven or eight smaller containers replaced boxes with divided interiors. As with wooden desk boxes, the wooden storage container gradually lost out to the tin boxes that proliferated after 1800.

After 1875, lithography could be used to decorate tin, and manufacturers of tobacco, soap, and biscuits sold their wares around the world packed in tins decorated with catchy multi-colored labels. In the years before World War II, English biscuit tins were produced in many familiar shapes, from realistic castles to animals, clowns, and historic houses. Cheaper cardboard boxes slowly began to replace tin for food packaging by the second half of the nineteenth century. By World War II, biscuit tins pretty much disappeared, but tin continued to hold food in the familiar tin can, which actually was made of iron plated with tin.

North American Indian Boxes

In the beginning, according to the mythic tradition of the Northwest coast Indians, there was only darkness. The great chief

mid-nineteenth century, cylindrical tin wall boxes with hinged covers replaced wooden candle boxes. Candles were also sometimes stored in the tills of chests, in the hope that the tallow would guard against moths. Tinderboxes made of tin held flint that, when struck against a steel striker, created a spark to ignite tinder (often linen or wood shavings) that was also stored in the box. Some had lids to extinguish the tinder if necessary, while others were fitted with a socket for a candle on top.

Before the days of glass jars and tin cans, the pantry was filled with numerous round of the sky stored the moon and the sun in special boxes in his longhouse high in the heavens. Raven heard the rumors of these treasures and was curious. Watching the fortress, he saw the chief's daughter leave each day to draw water from a stream. One day, turning himself into a hemlock needle, he floated gently down into her cup. Soon the girl became pregnant and gave birth to a baby. The grandfather doted on the infant, even though he thought maybe its eyes looked a bit like a sly raven.

The child was prone to temper tantrums and demanded to play with the box that held the moon. Grandfather relented and before he knew it, Raven had released the moon into the heavens. Throwing another tantrum, the boy would not be quiet until grandfather gave him the larger box containing the sun. Raven immediately changed himself back into a bird and flew off with the prize through the open smoke hole in the roof. Soon tiring of his load, Raven stopped to rest. Chasing after him, the chief almost caught the trickster, but at the last moment, rather than give up the sun, Raven flung the box into the sky and there was light. To this day, the Indians of the Northwest Coast store their cherished possessions in carved wooden boxes.

Different Indian tribes from Alaska to New England made boxes. They had pretty much the same use, as storage containers for food and personal items that European and American boxes had. However, they differed in the materials employed and in their distinct decoration. After their exposure to Europeans in the mid-eighteenth century, the Eskimos or Inuit Indians in Alaska used

Japanned, Chinese export tea chest with mother-of-pearl inlay holding two paktong (an alloy of nickel, zinc, and copper) containers, one for green tea and one for black. The accompanying will of Benjamin and Hannah Warrington in Virginia dated 1857 designates the chest for their daughter, Kezia.

ivory from prehistoric mammoths or walrus tusks to fashion small boxes for needles and snuff. Because of the absence of trees in the Arctic, wooden boxes were rare but a few driftwood boxes for tools, sewing supplies, and tobacco have survived. Like the ivory ones, they were often carved in the shape of a seal or walrus.

The Haida, Tlingit, Tsimshian, and Kwakiutl Indians living along the Northwest Coast of North America produced quite different boxes. Many of them were made for the feasting and exchange of gifts that characterized their great potlatch ceremonies. The best boxes were constructed of cedar, decorated with incised carving, inlaid with abalone shell, and then painted. The boxes were made of a single plank with three kerfs cut into the board so that it could be steam-bent into the shape of a rectangular box and

Mid-nineteenth century yellow pine wall box from Virginia's Shenandoah Valley constructed with pegs joining the sides and the bottom in the German tradition. These boxes were usually hung by the fire to keep the salt that was often stored in them dry.

Special Purpose Boxes

Although boxes to store household goods or personal items were the most common, boxes were made to contain every other conceivable item. For example, itinerate painters in the nineteenth century packed their colors, palettes, brushes, and combs for graining in distinctive artist boxes. Doctors carried their instruments in specially fitted boxes. Spectacles were carried in cases frequently covered in shagreen, to protect them. Calling-card cases, many imported from China, played an important role in the Victorian ritual of calling on friends and neighbors. Until the advent of modern day voting machines, ballots were deposited in ballot boxes. Over the centuries, boxes have been designed to hold countless games that have amused humankind since the beginning of time.

The number of boxes was limited only by what could be put into them. A late-nineteenth century box carved and decorated by the Chippewa Indians of Wisconsin held several eagle feathers used as a headdress. One of the most unusual boxes was one designed to transport the queen bee along with the rest of the hive. Then there were the boxes made as gifts by loggers in New England, carved out of a single piece of spruce in the shape of a book, to hold the spruce sap that they chewed like gum. Even stranger was the alabaster box from Tutankhamen's tomb that contained two hair balls wrapped in linen, which some speculate may have had something to do with a contract.

then either fastened together at the open corner with pegs or laced up with cedar roots. Smaller boxes were made of ivory and carved with stylized bear, owl, raven, and killer whale images, all of which played a part in their cultural mythology.

In the Midwestern United States, the Chippewa and Kickapoo tribes made baskets of locally grown birch bark or from beech and maple that they decorated with hieroglyphic-like figures and inlaid bone or shells from mussels found in local rivers. In addition to birch bark boxes, the Micmac, Algonquin, and Iroquois tribes of the Northeast also made burled fetish boxes. Boxes to hold personal items were fabricated from porcupine quills that were dyed and sewn to birch bark cases. Even today, many of these Indian tribes continue their ancient box-making traditions by selling souvenirs to tourists.

Into the 20th Century

By the twentieth century, handmade boxes fell out of favor as large factories met the demand for containers. Food was now stored in glass bottles, plastic jars, or cardboard boxes. If we want to store something, it is usually in a cardboard box or a plastic container. We write at desk computers or laptops, not elegant wooden lap desks.

As bathrooms became an essential component of twentieth century homes, dressing boxes largely disappeared as most men and women stored their body care products in wall cabinets or on the sink counter. Still, dressing cases or cosmetic boxes do survive. Rainer Facklam, a furniture maker in New York, sold a travel vanity that sat in a finely crafted stand with aluminum frame and ebony drawer fronts veneered in ash and pear wood. The aluminum travel case was fitted with the most stylish brands such as Chanel makeup, a Louis Vuitton address book, French perfumes, and a Mont Blanc pen. Unusual additions to the ensemble were a wine stopper, corkscrew, a pair of napkins, and six votive candles. Not many travel cases were so well equipped, but in this day of cheap travel, the travel case still does serve a useful purpose.

Jewelry and trinket boxes survive in even greater numbers, though most are made in China. More than a thousand Chinese manufacturers advertise their work on the Internet. Few of these boxes are made of wood and even fewer are handmade. Most are cast from zinc, pewter, aluminum, or plastic. Many manufacturers are obviously familiar with the heyday of box making in the eighteenth century, as their boxes are also made in myriad shapes from animals such as frogs, fish, and deer, to butterflies, owls, and even shrimp and snails that characterized the eighteenth century originals. They also come in the shape of twentieth-century objects, such as old-time telephones, cars, women's purses and high-heel shoes, the latter presumably a takeoff on the eighteenth century boot-shaped snuffboxes. One manufacturer specializes in heart-shaped boxes. Jewel boxes in the shape of Fabergé eggs are also popular, even though the originals only contained elegant surprises integral to the design and were not made to hold personal possessions. For the purest box enthusiast, another Chinese manufacturer's Website features numerous reproductions of historic boxes, but cast in metal or plastic rather than handmade with precious materials.

With the exception of decorative boxes for special uses, most modern boxes are made of solid or woven plastic, cardboard, or tin, and are designed for specific utilitarian purposes. Document boxes still exist, but they take the form

An unusually large, early nineteenth century, grain-painted box, probably made in Maryland or Pennsylvania, with a sliding lid typical of candle boxes.

of plastic boxes, metal-filing cases, or simple cardboard boxes with no tops. Plastic organizers provide specialized compartments for the detritus that clutters the modern desk.

In some quarters, jewelry boxes have morphed into something entirely unexpected. When compact discs became popular in the early 1980s, the Polygram record division of Philips Electric designed a thin, plastic box to hold them based loosely on the familiar plastic audiocassette box developed in the 1960s. They soon became known as jewel cases, not because they held anything rare—in 1990 alone, nearly 300 million were made—but because the hinge on the case worked like the arbors in watches that spin on tiny jewels.

The box-making tradition survives today, if largely as an art form. Since World War II and the resurgence of handcraftsmanship, the interest in fine boxes has grown. Many of the same craftsmen who turned their skills to making studio furniture in the 1960s have also on occasion made boxes. But box specialists make some of the finest boxes. This is a field unto itself. Similarly, a subset of woodturners also produces turned boxes with the purpose of containing something. If the turning has a wide mouth and a lid, it can hold an object, as opposed to a turned vessel with a narrow mouth and usually no lid that is designed for show. In the eighteenth and nineteenth centuries many boxes were turned out of both wood and metal, but by and large they were utilitarian and plain. Today, however, turning has evolved into a high art, and turned boxes are among the most creative containers.

Boxes and Their Makers

The box makers represented in this book were selected to participate in an exhibition that opened in September 2009 at the Messler Gallery of the Center for Furniture Craftsmanship (CFC) in Rockport, Maine. A three-person jury made the selections: myself; Toni Sikes, founder of *Guild.com*; and Kevin Wallace, the noted writer on craft and woodturning. The exhibition is scheduled to travel for two or three years, to a variety of museums across the United States.

The brief for the exhibit was simple. The box must be able to contain something, be made of wood, and be small enough to sit on a table. The boxes ranged in size from two or three inches in diameter to over three feet tall. About a third of the boxes were made by full-time box makers, another third by woodturners, and the rest by furniture artists. All were made of wood, and even the one turned in elk horn by Kip Christensen included a turned ring of ebony that contained turquoise beads. One box by Bonnie Bishoff and J. M. Syron featured colorful polymer clay as a veneer over a wooden frame.

A sculptor produced one box and two of the turners considered themselves sculptors as well. Couples produced three of the entries, while one was a collaborative effort. In addition to the women in the four collaborations, five more women are represented in the exhibit. Although the majority of the makers were American, three were British, two Canadian, two Australian, one French, one German, and one Japanese. About two-thirds of the makers were self-taught, while the others trained mostly at

Rhode Island School of Design, Rochester Institute of Technology, or the Boston University Program in Artisany, which operated from 1985 until 1995.

Most of the full-time box makers produce a variety of forms, from simple production pieces to highly complex, one-of-a-kind examples. Turners seemed to alternate between making vessels and lidded containers. Cabinetmakers made boxes as a break from larger furniture forms, and as a way of experimenting with ideas in small scale.

Not surprisingly, most of the box makers and the furniture makers, such as Peter Lloyd, produced finely crafted square or rectangular boxes in the tradition of jewelry or document boxes. Two of the boxes took the shape of an oval—also a common shape from the nineteenth century. Although round boxes were another conventional shape, the circular box by Emi Ozawa has no historical precedent. Of course, most of the turned boxes tend to be circular in cross section, but it is easy to miss that the bugs by Louise Hibbert and Jim Christiansen started out on a lathe.

Throughout history, the most exquisite boxes were made of precious materials such as silver and gold, while wooden boxes were more utilitarian. Many boxes of wood, such as dressing cases and lap desks, were made during the eighteenth century, but by the nineteenth century, wooden boxes tended to be made for specific utilitarian uses such as storage or shipping. The tradition of fine wooden boxes as luxury items was not revived until the second half of the twentieth century.

ABOVE TOP

Mid-nineteenth century chest displaying three different graining techniques, attributed to Jonathan Poff of Wrightsville, Pennsylvania. It may have held his graining supplies while also serving as a sample of his work.

ABOVE BOTTOM

Mid-nineteenth century treenware, turned box. Ornamental turning in the nineteenth century was a precursor of the turning revival in the mid-twentieth century.

Early nineteenth century watch hutches carved from solid blocks of wood, (left) American in mahogany, (right) English in ebony, with inlaid and applied ivory decoration. People believed that pocket watches must be stored vertically when not in use to ensure accurate timekeeping.

These twentieth century boxes, like their predecessors, depend largely on exotic woods for their appeal. Robert Ingham contrasted figured ebony with pear, and Andrew Crawford set wavy amboyna against dyed sycamore. Po Shun Leong employed sixteen different woods, some of which he enhanced with paint or gilding. A few, such as the boxes of the Seatons and Ulrike Scriba, were embellished with metal fittings, the former with copper, and the latter with embossed silver. Philip Weber's boxes have delicate silver inlay, and Scriba's are made with complex marquetry. Most of the turned boxes also depend on exotic woods for their overall effect.

However, one of the cabinetmakers, Andy Buck, produced a box in the shape of a

duck. Although he was following in a long tradition of boxes in the shape of animals, the scale of his duck—twenty inches high—was unusual. Also in the eighteenth century tradition of boxes in the shapes of animals are the weevil by Hibbert and the beetle by Christensen. Kim Kelzer's box in the shape of an iron and Craig Nutt's tea caddy in the shape of a tea pot had more in common with twentieth century Pop Art. Leong has developed a distinctive assemblage style that has virtually no historical precedent.

Because rich wood has long signified luxury, it is surprising that almost half of the boxes are painted. Tom Loeser pioneered the embellishment of wood with paint. In the case of Yuji Kubo's lacquered box, the decoration also connotes luxury. In some cases, such as the bugs of Christensen and Hibbert, the duck by Buck, and the tea caddy by Nutt, paint is necessary to complete the transformation of the wood into another being. In the case of Tommy Simpson, the surface of his toolbox has been transformed into an abstract landscape painting, and Jenna Goldberg has wrapped her boxes in dazzling patterns. In the case of Jacques Vesery, painted carving has transformed the wood into a three-dimensional painting.

Most traditional turned boxes took the form of simple cylinders. Lids were added to vase-shaped vessels. It was an easy leap to add a turned top to a turned vase-shaped vessel, making it into a box. Common in the nineteenth century, these turned boxes were more ornamental than useful, but they were still boxes. The cylindrical boxes of Andrew

Potocnik and Richard Raffan follow in this tradition.

Traditional turned boxes were a staple of the early twentieth century hobby turners, but by the end of the century turning became increasingly complex. The turned form became pierced as in the work of Hans Weissflog, or undulating, as in the work of Michael Mode, who also added complexity by using various laminated woods cut into patterns. Steven Kennard combined several different shapes in a single composition. Although the O'Rourkes turn traditional vase shapes, they embellish the turnings by adding unusual carved details such as flowers or animals. Michael Hosaluk produces highly organic shapes with his segmented turning techniques. Jacques Vesery simply uses the turned form as a canvas for his carving and coloring. Although the boxes by Ray Jones are turned, he considers himself exclusively a box maker.

Several boxes took amorphous shapes. The carved work by Jean-Christophe Couradin, a sculptor, looks like a stone eroded by running water. The segmented turnings of Hosaluk suggest some amorphous creatures. Michael Cullen's box is an abstract landscape.

All of the makers chose the box form because of the possibility of enticing the viewer to interact with it. By its nature, a box demands to be opened and filled with personal treasures. Bonnie Klein and Jacques Vesery already have filled their boxes with symbols of the seasons. Leong created a secret compartment that cannot be found without opening specific drawers. The makers who featured the wood invariably sanded the surface to a silky finish that invited the viewer to caress the box, if for no other reason than simple tactile pleasure.

Because the first hunter/gathers began to collect things, they invented boxes in which to store them. Over the centuries, the box has evolved into many specialized forms to hold every conceivable object. Today, objects and their containers overwhelm us and we even rent off-site storage in which to hold them. However, the handcrafted boxes in this book are in another category. They are the result of countless hours of highly skilled labor, creative talent, and imagination. In the process, the makers have left their unique fingerprints and a bit of their soul in their boxes.

These artists speak with their hands and we are inspired to listen.

This Victorian puzzle box is dated 1879. Solving the puzzle frees deposited coins.

BONNIE BISHOFF
J.M. SYRON

(Bonnie) Born: 1963, Philadelphia Pennsylvania
(J.M.) Born: 1960, Columbus, Ohio

Bringing Two Mediums Together

It is all about sharing, which they have been doing since 1987. For Bonnie Bishoff and J.M. Syron, their collaboration is what makes their work distinctive. Both have their own sensibilities, which combine to create a singular expression. They like to make things together and neither could think of doing it alone. There is a certain division of labor—he does most of the construction and she does most of the carving and polymer clay. Their designs, which may percolate for up to a year before coming to fruition, merge their ideas.

Neither was formally trained to make furniture. In high school, Syron began an apprenticeship with a musical instrument maker while also attending West Chester Community College in a tool and die-making program. Before graduating, he shifted goals and apprenticed for two years with a furniture maker in Charleston, South Carolina, and then worked as

"Our work is a lot about melding things, partly because we're collaborating, but we're also bringing two mediums together," says Bishoff.

a foreman in a reproduction shop in Boston. While working on her degree in science at Oberlin College in Ohio, Bishoff learned woodblock printing and worked as a carpenter's assistant, building theater sets.

Making is in their genes. Bishoff's grandfather was a tool-and-die maker, and she still uses his tools. Her

ABOVE
Bonnie Bishoff and J.M. Syron in their studio.

OPPOSITE
Inner Eye Box, 2008. Bird's-eye maple, basswood, polymer clay; H. 9" W. 18" D. 9".

RIGHT

Woodland Shade Vessel, 2004. Walnut, polymer clay; H. 11" W. 17" D. 10". *Woodland Shade Vessel* relates to the *Islesboro* series, and the pattern in the clay body grew out of an interest in ornamental hostas.

BELOW

Sea and Sky Altar Coffer, 2006. Mahogany, polymer clay; H. 26" W. 27" D. 19". Based on a ceremonial coffer, *Sea and Sky Altar Coffer* was made for the 2007 *Inspired by China* exhibit. It holds Lakota Indian prayer ties that Bishoff used in a healing ceremony after spinal surgery. The "cracked ice" latticework and the wave and cloud forms on the exterior are traditional Chinese motifs.

mother, a tailor, was the model of patience. Syron's fiber artist mother gave him a love of texture and pattern. Their children made wooden swords in the shop before moving on to building bicycle ramps and jumps. Their older son, who is considering a career in industrial design, also helps in the shop.

Bishoff and Syron met on Martha's Vineyard where they were both doing carpentry, she fresh out of college and he taking a break from furniture. They married and settled in Philadelphia where she taught science in a Quaker school, and he ran a production shop. In 1987, they began to design furniture and eventually, Syron started his own high-end custom woodworking business while the couple continued to develop their own designs. Seven years and two children later, they took the big leap: Bishoff quit her job to work full-time in their craft business, and they moved to Rockport on the coast just north of Boston.

With an architect friend from Philadelphia who has a design/build company, they share a shop in an old industrial building in nearby Gloucester. Depending on the workload, they employ up to three people and occasionally accept an apprentice. About half of their work is custom remolding, often for their furniture clients.

They make a range of furniture including tables, lamps, seating, and vessels, including boxes and vases. Bishoff alternates between embellishing their furniture with carving or with polymer clay. Her inspirations are nature, Native American carving, and Art Nouveau. Bears dance on the splats of a series of chairs and settees. The carved façade of their *Islesboro Small Chest,* which would have been at home during the Art Nouveau craze of the late-nineteenth century, suggests a swirling maelstrom.

Bishoff's polymer clay motifs, with names like honeycomb, trillium, dandelion, ginkgo, and autumn foliage, take their cue from nature. Although their fish lamps (*Brook Trout* and *Holy Mackerel*) employ the clay in three dimensions, mostly it is used as a veneer. The oval-shaped *Java Credenza* and the curved back of the *Star Chair* show off the clay to good effect. Sometimes they combine both carving and polymer clay in one piece, as on their *Otter Chairs,* with carving on the back or arms and polymer clay on the seat rails.

Using polymer clay for veneer is unique in the craft world. In the early 1990s, an art teacher friend showed Bishoff a book about the material, and she began to experiment.

Sun and Shade Wall Hung Cabinet, 2006. Walnut, polymer clay; H. 26" W. 20" D. 12". Essentially a functional painting, *Sun and Shade Wall Hung Cabinet* was inspired by antique Japanese theater kimonos with botanical patterns and color blocks.

Bishoff rolls the polymer clay through an industrial-size pasta machine and then colors, slices, folds, stretches, and combines it into an infinite number of patterns. She appropriates the same millefiori (millions of flowers) and other techniques glass makers use to produce multi-colored patterns in glass. Clay is much easier to manipulate than glass because it does not have to be kept molten. Porcelain makers used the same techniques in the eighteenth and early nineteenth centuries as did Damascene sword makers, who distorted and sliced steel at low angles to create wavy patterns. The chatoyant patterns in the clay are similar to those in wood.

The couple started the *Inner Eye* series (named for the shape of the box) in 2004. Even if customers did not want a large piece of furniture, they could always find room for a box. Syron and Bishoff had actually made some boxes early in their career—large ones influenced by Northwest Coast Haida and Tlingit ceremonial boxes. Bishoff likes the idea of boxes as ceremonial containers for special occasions.

Inner Eye is both carved and veneered. The base is carved in a Japanese wave pattern and then painted with metallic lacquer to make it pop. The curved body, ideal for showing off the clay patterns, is made with thin, bendable plywood vacuum-pressed over a form. The laminated sides are then glued to flanges at each end. Once the one-sixteenth-inch-thick sheets of clay have been fired, they can be cut, sanded, and applied like veneer. Because clay is not as brittle as wood, it is easier to work, but assembly can be tricky because hammers and clamps can

ABOVE TOP

Winter Woods Coffer, 2006. Walnut, cherry, polymer clay; H. 18" W. 22" D. 16". Winter walks in the snow are always an inspiration. *Winter Woods Coffer* was constructed during a howling winter blizzard.

ABOVE BOTTOM

Persian Box, 2004. Cherry, polymer clay; H. 6" W. 8" D. 8". Named after the domed roofs of ancient Persia, *Persian Box* was an early attempt at something small, functional, collectable, and unique in its use of polymer clay.

crack the material. All parts are finished before assembly because the lacquer would mar the clay. The underside of the lid and the interior are finished with maple veneer. Because a thick piece of clay tends to crack when fired, Bishoff had been sculpting a thin sheet of clay around aluminum foil to make handles, but recently she has started to use less dense clay that does not crack.

Bishoff sums it up: "Our work is a lot about melding things, partly because we're collaborating, and we're bringing two circles of ideas together, but we're also bringing two mediums together." It is this melding of two minds, two hands, and two materials that produces their unique homage to nature.

ABOVE

Java Credenza, 2002. Mahogany, pommele sapeli, polymer clay; H. 38" W. 56" D. 24". *Java Credenza* was the couple's first attempt at creating a large case piece using polymer clay veneers. The piece recalls French Art Deco furniture.

ABOVE

Pumpkin Box, 2004. Mahogany, polymer clay; H. 7" Dia. 7". Summer and winter squash served as a model for *Pumpkin Box*, their first box made by molding polymer clay around a form.

ANDY BUCK

Born: 1966, Baltimore, Maryland

Listening to Nature

Andy Buck's *Mr. Red* is only twenty inches high while Martin Puryer's *Lever # 1* stands over eleven feet, but they both have a similar form and a common inspiration. After seeing Puryer's abstract wooden sculpture dating from the late-1980s, Buck learned that a duck had influenced the sculptor. Also interested in the duck form, Buck created a bench with similar proportions called *Lemonhead-Decoy #1*. Soon after, he trekked to the Havre de Grace Decoy Museum in Maryland to study the decoys for himself.

As usual, Buck started with only a sketch, editing the design as he went along. He describes the process as "thinking with his hands."

Gunners, the real decoys hunters use to attract ducks, caught his fancy, rather than the more realistic show pieces. He appreciated the decoys' patina of wear and age, a characteristic of his own work. And he liked the idea of attraction—that these decoys might attract real birds, just as his work might be attractive to people. In 2003, he made a series of decoy sculptures for the Wexler Gallery in Philadelphia and experienced his first sell-out show.

Buck had crafted his first duck box on a whim. He painted it black with shades of blue and gave it a sharp yellow beak. Although principally a furniture maker, he has produced many boxes during his career and thinks of his cabinets as just big boxes. His first ones, featuring

ABOVE

A self-portrait of Andy Buck in his studio located near his home in Honeoye Falls, New York.

OPPOSITE

Mr. Red, 2008. Mahogany, ebony; H. 20" W. 20" D. 6".

ABOVE LEFT

Decoys, 2003. Walnut, mahogany, poplar; H. 21" W. 14" D. 9". Two of a series of twenty-seven birds Buck carved for an exhibition.

ABOVE RIGHT

Lemonhead Bench, 2002. Poplar; H. 62" W. 72" D. 18". This was Buck's first decoy even though it is more than five feet high. It is equipped with his familiar perforated spoon shape that could be a satellite dish, ears, cupped hands, or maybe the whole thing is a strange raft with a little sail.

traditional dovetails with sliding tops or hinged lids, were produced as Christmas presents. He also has made some band-sawn boxes, humidors, and at least one box in the shape of an arrowhead.

Buck's friend, New Hampshire furniture maker Jere Osgood, started him thinking about inside and outside space; what the cabinet, or box, would contain; and how that would affect the form. Although *Black and White with Broom,* a cabinet from early in his career, focused on a utilitarian tool in a container, it also explored the dichotomy between the inside and the outside. This concept is repeated more subtly in his recent furniture like *Watermelon Table,* which has a top formed by two halves of the sliced melon, and his *Dot Bench,* with a seat that

suggests a peanut laid open to reveal what is inside.

Mr. Red was fashioned out of several pieces of laminated mahogany, which is good for carving. As usual, Buck started with only a sketch, editing the design as he went along. He describes the process as "thinking with (his) hands." All of the parts, including the beak, the head, the neck, and the body, were joined with mortise-and-tenon joints. The cavity in the duck's body was shaped with carving gouges to produce a smooth interior with a rounded bottom edge. He picked ebony for the hinge and the knob to lift the lid.

Sanding through several coats of milk paint exposed traces of the red mahogany and created the weathered finish. Buck's

Photo by Bruce Miller

muted color palette is influenced by artist, Paul Klee, who believed color could touch the spirit in the same way music does. Some of Buck's furniture, such as *Figaro Bench*, a bench that takes the shape of a cello, has a direct musical reference. Buck hopes his furniture will transform an interior space the way music changes the mood of an environment.

Weathered finishes and folk references recall the handmade objects his father, who worked for the World Heath Organization, brought back from trips to Africa, Indonesia, and New Guinea. Although the specific African references of his early furniture have largely disappeared, some of his latest pieces still contain these allusions. Although the half-circles on *Scallop Bench*,

for example, clearly recall the shellfish, the painted and carved seat also evokes an African shield.

As a political science student at Virginia Commonwealth University in Richmond, Buck stumbled into woodworking when he needed some art credits. After graduation, Buck worked for a year on Capitol Hill as a congressional aide. Yearning to make things, he quit and took a job in a cabinet shop but soon realized he needed formal training if he wanted to do more than run a router all day. He spent a year in the Southeastern Massachusetts University program before going on to earn his master's degree in fine arts at Rhode Island School of Design. Since 1999, he has taught at Rochester Institute of Technology, where he is an

Dot Bench, 2007. Poplar, rosewood; H. 17" W. 60" D. 18". The peanut-shaped seat is inlaid with rosewood dots that suggest the texture of a peanut shell. A client in Aspen, Colorado, wanted a bench that could also double as a table.

Photo by Brian Powell

Blossfeldt Chairs, 1996. Mahogany, wool fabric; H. 30" W. 36" D. 15". These chairs were made for a show at the Clark Gallery in Lincoln, Massachusetts. The upholstery accentuates the hand-carved scrolls.

associate professor in the School for American Crafts.

Teaching challenges Buck to find new solutions to problems his students encounter, and it motivates him to produce his own body of work to set a good example. Buck segregates his personal work from his students' work and maintains a studio he recently built near his home in Honeoye Falls, New York.

Botanical forms and animals that abound in the woods around his shop influence many of Buck's designs. He finds a similar inspiration in the photographs of Karl Blossfeldt, the early twentieth century photographer who did stunning, close-up portraits of nature. The curved ends of his *Blossfeldt Bench* suggest fiddlehead ferns. More

Teaching challenges Buck to find new solutions to problems his students encounter, and it motivates him to produce his own body of work to set a good example.

recently, the stylized vines and pompons on a headboard, *Cattail Hat Rack*, and *Pod Table*, with a peapod-shaped top and legs, are other nods to nature.

Tools, which he believes define a culture, also have been a continuing source of inspiration. Some of Buck's early efforts featured found metal tools. A series of wall hangings called *Rehandled Tools* had a more direct tool reference. It consisted of found shovels, hammers, pitchforks, and other implements he fitted with sculptural handles painted in bright colors. He further refined the concept with a collection of everyday objects like *Mr. Clean*, a toilet brush, and turned wooden toilet plungers he transformed into art. More recently, his series of *Totems* are sculptural shapes that allude to specific functional objects.

During the past year, Buck has expanded his horizons to include the construction of a nursery as well as a Calderesque mobile and toys for his newborn baby boy. All of a sudden, he has begun to look more closely at toys, tree forts, birdhouses, and go-carts, and is already thinking about ways to combine these objects with furniture.

Photo by Bruce Miller

ABOVE

Lily Side Table, 2008. Cherry, rosewood; H. 25" W. 18" D. 16". After seeing water lilies in bloom, Buck was inspired to make this table. For him, the rosewood dots recall the bursts of light when sun strikes the water on a summer day.

LEFT

Black and White with Broom, 1993. Ash, copper, bristle; H. 69" W. 21" D. 12". The writings of Joseph Campbell on the power of myth inspired this cabinet. Examining the ritual of cleaning, Buck deifies the common broom.

KIP CHRISTENSEN

Born: 1955, Preston, Indiana

To Get Good Ideas, Start with Many Ideas

Kip Christensen claims not to be a professional turner—he is an educator with a long-standing passion for woodturning. After earning his bachelor and master's degrees in industrial education from Brigham Young University, he taught for two years at Humboldt State University in Arcata, California. In 1988, he joined the faculty at Brigham Young University and has been there ever since. At Brigham Young, Christensen teaches woodworking and furniture design, and mentors technology education majors doing their student teaching. Although a few of his students become furniture makers, most go on to careers in technology and engineering education.

"If someone doesn't find turning to be fun, they are probably not doing it right," *Christensen says.*

Even with his strong academic background, Christensen has had a lifetime of exposure to hands-on woodworking. As a first grader in Idaho, he remembers fishing pencil stubs out of the wood stove in the schoolhouse and making his own pencils. He recovered the lead and stuck it into the soft pith of freshly cut willow sticks. In junior high, he began helping his father in the family-owned kitchen cabinet factory. While studying for his undergraduate degree, he continued to work in the company designing and selling.

Photo by Scott Finlayson.

ABOVE

Kip Christensen at his lathe in 2008. For him, turning is fun, fluid and therapeutic. He takes great satisfaction in transforming a discarded log or a piece of firewood into an object of lasting beauty and utility.

OPPOSITE

Antler Box, 2007. Elk antler, turquoise, African blackwood; H. 2½" Dia. 3½".

ABOVE

Tower Box, 2007. Box elder burl, blackwood, amboyna burl; H. 7" Dia. 2¾". "Form comes first," says Christensen. "There seems to be no other quality that has the power to compensate for poor form." The graceful *Tower Box* proves the point.

Christensen first experienced turning while peeling off some fresh green cherry shavings in a college woodworking class. He felt he had discovered something truly special. He became permanently hooked after helping out at the first Utah Woodturning Symposium in 1979. The symposium gave Christensen a chance to meet some of the best turners in the world. From that small beginning, the conference now attracts more than 500 participants and celebrates its thirtieth anniversary in 2009. For nine of those years, Christensen served as the organizer, after his colleague and symposium founder, Dale Nish, retired. It is recognized as the longest running woodturning symposium in the world.

ABOVE TOP

Whited Sepulchre, 2004. Russian olive burl; H. 5" Dia. 6". The *Whited Sepulchre* series was born after a family trip to Bryce Canyon, Utah, where Christensen was inspired by the natural texture of the land. Portions of the surface have been sanded, sandblasted, and bleached.

ABOVE BOTTOM

Inlaid Box, 2003. Box elder burl, blackwood; H. 3" Dia. 4½". *Inlaid Box* features a delicate ring of blackwood highlighting the figure in the box elder burl. The simplicity of the design belies the steps necessary to ensure dimensional stability. The wood is roughed out, dried, re-roughed out, and dried again to ensure it is stable.

Typical of most turners, Christensen started with bowls and vessels, but he lavishes the most time on the surface finish rather than on the turning itself. His *Whited Sepulchre* series, for example, has only a shallow depression in the top to suggest a container and is more tactile than functional. He subjects the surface to a series of controlled abuses such as sandblasting, bleaching, and sanding to achieve a complex, mottled effect.

Throughout his career, Christensen has honed his turning skills by making thousands of tops—the kind that spin by twisting a stem with two fingers. Early in his career he offered a couple of dozen to a gallery, and within a few weeks came an order for a thousand more. The orders have never stopped. Now his son, Preston, who has been turning since elementary school, has taken over the task of filling some of the requests for more tops.

Christensen is a versatile turner, but is best known for his lidded containers. His interest in boxes stems from exposure to the work of the turner and box maker Del Stubbs, who attended the Utah symposiums in the late-1970s and early 1980s. Christensen was impressed with how precise and challenging a box could be. From a design standpoint, the base and the lid have to function well together. The lid obviously needs to fit, but should it fit loosely and come off easily; fit tightly to open with a crisp popping sound; or somewhere in between? Tiny changes in diameter make a big difference. And boxes need to be made for use and not to feel as if they might break when handled.

Polymer Clay Spinning Tops, 2003. Polymer clay; H. 1½" Dia. 2". Christensen has turned many thousands of spinning tops during his career and has recently experimented with polymer clay in collaboration with Judy Belcher.

Christensen is recognized as the first craftsman to turn boxes from elk antlers. The lathe is an ancient tool so it is possible someone once turned bowls from elk burrs, but he has never seen one. Beginning in the 1970s, several other turners were making wooden bowls with natural edges, but none used antler. Christensen was looking at the burr at the base of a rack of elk antlers and saw the possibilities for a bowl with a natural edge. After turning a few antler bowls, he began to make them with lids and then gradually added ornament.

Christensen has experimented with cow bone, and deer, caribou, and moose antlers, but prefers elk because of the range of colors—maroon, gray, and black—that the others lack. He buys the antlers from dealers who collect them in the wild after the animals shed them each year. The burrs need to be custom cut from the antler.

Turning antler is both laborious and tricky. The center is porous, so after turning it for awhile, he applies cyanoacrylate glue to fill the pores and turns some more—repeating the process several times. He could turn it soft, but it would not sand evenly. Further complicating the process is the fact that the antler stinks when turning it, and the dust is said to be carcinogenic. Christensen must wear an air-filtering helmet.

Christensen leaves the underside of the lid slightly thicker at the center than at the sides, so the round tenon at the base of the finial can fit into a hole without penetrating the underside. The bowl rests on a delicate turned bead. He has experimented with

ABOVE TOP

*Miscellaneous Antler Pieces,*1997. Elk antler, ebony, pink ivory wood; H. 2½" Dia. ¾". Christensen's first *Antler* series began as simple shallow bowls. A natural edge came next, followed by a contrasting ring of blackwood or pink ivory wood embellished with small turquoise beads.

ABOVE BOTTOM

Lidded Box, 1995. Macassar ebony; H. 1¾" Dia. 3". Form is paramount. In *Lidded Box*, the shape of the body echoes the shape of the lid, which in turn is shaped for ease of removal. Note how the light sapwood on the base is perfectly proportioned with the sapwood exposed on the lid.

chatterwork among other methods, to create a decorative band around the bowl, to accent the line where the lid meets the base.

Christensen likes to insert a turned ring in a contrasting wood such as African blackwood set with small stones beads. He

---

Christensen has experimented with deer, caribou, moose antlers, and cow bone, but prefers elk.

---

has experimented with man-made tiger's eye and pink coral, but likes turquoise best because of the bold, contrasting colors. The handmade beads vary slightly so he can pick just the right sizes to avoid any gaps.

Ever the teacher, Christensen has made few boxes in the last couple of years. Recently, developing instructional videos for turners has occupied most of his free time. He and his colleague, Rex

Burningham, have identified sixty projects that will give aspiring artists the basics of turning. So far, about half have been filmed and released on DVDs.

But he never ceases thinking about boxes. He preaches that the best way to get good ideas is to develop many ideas. Instead of drawings, he often makes quick templates by sketching outlines on folded sheets of paper, which, when cut out, become full-scale silhouettes of new pieces. Christensen says, "If someone doesn't find turning to be fun, they are probably not doing it right." Known for his clean lines and exacting craftsmanship, Christensen has been an active participant in the modern renaissance of woodturning since the 1970s.

BELOW LEFT

Box, 1997. Blackwood, moose antler, turquoise; H. 2¾" Dia. 1¾". This box invites handling and close inspection. It required precision turning and flawless finishing.

BELOW RIGHT

Small Vessel and Bowl, 1997. Blackwood, turquoise; H. ¾" Dia. 3". The two pieces are linked in form as well as materials. Blackwood and turquoise are among Christensen's favorite materials.

JIM CHRISTIANSEN

Born: 1943, Ogden, Utah

Art Is Visual Therapy

In the mid-1990s, Jim Christiansen had what amounted to a mid-life crisis when he listened to his heart, gave up his career as a school administrator, and became a full-time wood turner. The seed may have been planted while Christiansen attended school in Nephi, Utah. He was not a good student, but his shop teacher, Dean Shaw, got him dreaming about a career as an artist. Even though his dad provided another role model as a carpenter who, in his words, "could split a pencil line with a handsaw," Christiansen just did not believe he had the talent.

For a person who values human relationships, it is odd Christiansen would choose bugs as a subject. But he says bugs can be quite beautiful and complex.

Instead of art school, Christiansen enlisted in the Air Force and learned to repair electronics on B-52 bombers. Afterward he enrolled in the University of Utah and earned his bachelor and master's degrees in special education. He then went on to Utah State for a doctorate in special education.

He later worked at Utah State and the University of Maine and was a school administrator in Wyoming and Idaho. It was a good living, but Christiansen could not ignore the urge to create. In 1985, he bought a Shopsmith and started making furniture as a hobby. He acquired an old Oliver lathe and taught himself turning.

ABOVE

Jim Christiansen works on a *Fossil* piece. Inlaying the carved fossil forms stretches his fine motor skills and requires extreme concentration.

OPPOSITE

Bob, 2008. Curly maple, ebony, wengé, brass; H. 12" W. 17" D. 10".

Spider Box, 2008. Ebony, maple, wengé, brass; H. 9" W. 13" D. 13". Christiansen's *Spider Box* was inspired by a ten-year old piece of African ebony. It is not an exact copy, but rather a sculptural interpretation of the essence of the black widow spider.

He took some art classes, and spent time with Cleve Taylor, a well-known caricature carver.

Then other role models entered his life. Christiansen attended a woodturning symposium and signed up for a workshop with Canadian turner, Michael Hosaluk. Christiansen was impressed with Michael's turning skills, but even more with his sense of humor and easy flow of creativity.

By 1996, he was turning full time in a studio he built adjacent to his house in Moscow, Idaho. For a small town, Moscow had a surprisingly vibrant arts community but only one other turner. The two helped each other and then others came to Christiansen's shop to learn. He now owns

Christiansen also embellishes his boxes with carvings of human figures. In the late-1990s, he started carving twisted roots that rose up from a base to hold his turned boxes. A few years later, he took the leap into figural carving.

six lathes and keeps his shop open twenty-four hours a day to accommodate anyone who wants to come. There is no charge—Christiansen believes that by giving, the gifts will come back.

It works. At any one time, he has five or six zealots, as he calls them, who want to become professional wood artists. It is not an apprenticeship program. He does

Root Box, 2008. Mallee burl, walnut, maple; H. 9"
Dia. 3½". One of a number of root box variations,
Root Box combines the formal turned box with
an organic root carving.

not teach but instead works with them as
colleagues. They learn by watching and he
answers questions, but the critiques are the
most important part of the relationship.
Traditionally, art students fear critiques, but
Christiansen thrives on them. Whenever
three or four students gather in the
shop, they discuss each other's work. By
responding to immediate feedback, the
students progress very quickly and their
work improves exponentially.

ABOVE TOP

Archaeopteryx Redux, 2008. Maple burl, eucalyptus
burl, walnut; H. 4½" Dia. 8". Adding carved fossil
bones, as in *Archaeopteryx Redux*, was an early
attempt by Christiansen to decorate his turnings.
Over the years, his fossils have gotten much
more realistic.

ABOVE BOTTOM

The Offering, 2006. Ribbon mahogany, maple;
H. 9" Dia. 15". For Christiansen, the three "bird skull"
figures in bondage in *The Offering* represent giving
and sacrifice, while the bowl holds things we offer
up to others.

Elusive Dreams, 2007.
Maple burl, maple;
H. 10" Dia. 9". The
potential of the good
things we visualize
inside *Elusive Dreams*
is somehow mitigated
by the sorrowful
figures that support
it. Reality tempers our
hopes and dreams.

across the ground. The article included photographs of actual beetles that he used as models.

Christiansen trimmed up the edges, fleshed out the form, and stuck it on a brass armature that suggested a pin, the traditional mounting for insects in specimen boxes. It sold quickly. Number two was more detailed and was stolen from a gallery. Number three was a black widow spider. *Bob* is even more detailed and painted with transparent, iridescent colors.

Christiansen carved the beetle's expression like a Mona Lisa smile to convey a sense of wry humor. It is not really smiling but is not unhappy, either. He was thinking of his son-in-law, Bob, who is similarly funny, hence the name for the box.

For a person who values human relationships, it is odd Christiansen would choose bugs as a subject. But he says bugs can be quite beautiful and complex. How do they move all those joints in their legs? How do they find their way? With such tiny brains, how do they learn the skills of their trade? What are they thinking? Mankind's fascination with bugs is part of the appeal of Christiansen's work.

Christiansen started out using richly figured burl, but later developed his own expression through his bug boxes and fossil vessels. The vessels evolved from a childhood curiosity about dinosaurs; the wood grain reminded him of soil that might contain buried dinosaur bones. That led to inlaying carved bones on his turned vessels to suggest fossils. Like his bug boxes, the fossils are not exact copies but rather are artistic suggestions.

Bob, Christiansen's fourth bug box, became more complex and realistic because of input from his students. The idea emerged from the wreckage of a bowl that blew up on his lathe. One of the pieces looked like a scarab beetle. About that time, he saw a magazine article about the reverence for a dung beetle as a god in ancient Egypt. In the myth, a giant dung beetle rolled the sun across the sky, just as earthly beetles roll bits of dung

Photo by Steve Sinner.

Christiansen also embellishes his boxes with carvings of human figures. In the late-1990s, he started carving twisted roots that rose up from a base to hold his turned boxes. A few years later, he took the leap into figural carving. The first one was a carved female nude that held aloft a box as if holding the world in her hands. A more emotion-laden work, called *Greed*, featured three figures—a woman holding a dead baby, a helmeted soldier, and a starving man—all shouldering a bowl topped with a handle in the shape of a stylized dollar sign.

Representing even darker emotions, *Thinking of You*, was supported on the shoulders of human figures with crows' heads. He conceived the piece soon after a speeding taxi seriously injured his son. The accident rekindled his childhood memory of raising crows as pets. One day a neighbor shot his crows for no reason, just as his son was almost killed in the accident for no reason.

Christiansen thinks of art as visual poetry that carries meaning beyond the individual words that make up the poem. He would like people to interact with his boxes in their own way and make connections that are meaningful to them. He hopes his art will allow people to experience new feelings, gain new insights, and make the world just a little better place. But even more, he revels in having developed skills he never thought possible and takes great pleasure in sharing those skills with others.

Photo by Will Simpson.

Photo by Stephen Hatcher.

JEAN-CHRISTOPHE COURADIN

Born: 1961, Dijon, France

Visual Emotions, Tactile Pleasures

Water Sculpture. It is unusual for Jean-Christophe Couradin to name his work because he wants viewers to bring their own narratives to the piece. In addition to the title, it is numbered K-29. Because he makes about a hundred pieces a year, he assigns one hundred numbers to each letter. Thus, this is his 1,129th piece since he began marking his work in 1998.

Couradin is not a furniture maker, nor a box maker, nor a turner. He is an artist who makes sculpture that is meant to interact with the viewer.

For Couradin, the title evokes rushing water over a rock; perhaps the waters of the Ouche and the Suzon rivers that come together and flow through his boyhood home in Dijon, France. But could it be the stylized head of a dolphin gliding through the ocean, or perhaps a helmeted biker speeding though the Alps? And then the top pivots open and the image is transformed. The viewer's focus shifts from the abstract shape to what could be inside the tiny box.

Couradin is not a furniture maker, nor a box maker, nor a turner. He is an artist who makes sculpture that is meant to interact with the viewer. The pieces that do not open as boxes nonetheless invite the viewer to touch and feel their smoothly polished curves. The rough-cut wood itself often suggests the final shape. He uses the traditional sculptor's arsenal of chisels, gouges, rasps,

ABOVE
Jean-Christophe Couradin in his home studio.

OPPOSITE
Water Sculpture, 2008. Madagascar rosewood; H. 7" W. 12" D. 8½".

ABOVE

Untitled, 2007. Honduran lignum vitae; H. 9¾"
W. 25¼" D. 11¾". Lignum vitae is one of the hardest
woods. Couradin uses only traditional chisels,
gouges, rasps, and scrapers—no power tools.

LEFT

Untitled, 2008. Mozambiquan ebony; H. 23½"
W. 11¾" D. 9¾". For a scientist this might conjure up
the complex folds of DNA. To a nature lover it would
evoke vines hanging from trees in a dense forest.

and scrapers to shape his abstract forms.
Each piece is then sanded and polished
with wax, using an old buffing tool that he
saw on a tour of a tobacco-pipe factory in
northeastern France.

During the thirteenth century, when
the Dukes of Burgundy took up residence
in Dijon, the city flourished as a cultural
and artistic center. But after the union of
Burgundy with France, the city lost its
cultural prominence. Following World
War II, it flourished as an industrial center.
Couradin's father worked as a technician
who installed X-ray machines around the
city. His son had little exposure to art, much
less woodworking.

Untitled, 2008. Brazilian rosewood; H. 9¾"
W. 19½" D. 15½".
Couradin's smaller sculptures can be set in a number of positions, achieving his goal of "variable geometry."

Then a chance encounter changed the course of his life. His sister and her American husband came visiting. The couple lost a wallet full of cash during their travels, and the family offered to help their son-in-law earn some money by making them a coffee table. A trained carpenter, he bought some simple tools and proceeded to fabricate some furniture. Couradin watched, helped, and found he liked that kind of work.

In 1979, at the age of eighteen, Couradin left home. He had shown the coffee table to some friends, who thought they could make a living reproducing it. He and his six companions moved to Trieves, a picturesque area of rolling farmland and forests surrounded by the French Alps about thirty miles from Grenoble. There, the group rented a house and set up a cooperative studio to begin making furniture.

After two years in the country, the group began to go their separate ways, so Couradin moved back to Dijon where he took jobs working in furniture and cabinetmaking shops, all the while refining his woodworking skills.

By 1984, Couradin began giving classes in a local woodworking program. While teaching there, he produced his first sculptures—chess sets—and he made his first wooden boxes to hold the pieces. These boxes were rustic affairs carved out of scrap wood, their lids decorated with two-dimensional carving and attached with leather hinges. He also began to produce card cases, pencil boxes, and wooden games to sell at local craft fairs.

In 1986, Couradin met his partner, and the next year the couple returned to the French Alps to live in the country not far from Grenoble. His partner, a psychologist, had gone to school there. They both love

Untitled, 2007. Lignum vitae; H. 9¾" W. 11¾" D. 7¾". Couradin started with boxes and moved on to sculpture, but most of his work still opens to expose tiny compartments.

the mountains and skiing. About six years ago, the family moved into the town of Le Touvet, where their two children had easier access to school. Working from a studio in his house, Couradin is inspired by the natural beauty of the Alps.

In 1989, Couradin visited Guiana, on the northeastern coast of South America. While in Guiana, he discovered the exotic woods that grew in the dense tropical forests.

When he returned to France he received his only art training, a couple of drawing and sculpture classes at the Ecole des Beaux-Arts in Grenoble. Almost overnight, the character of his work changed, from utilitarian items to sculpture.

His favorite woods now include highly figured lignum vitae from South America, cocobolo from Mexico, snakewood from Guiana, Macassar ebony, and pink ivory

Couradin was inspired by sculptor Henry Moore's metaphorical description of the tactile attraction of sculpture.

wood from South Africa, rosewood from Brazil, mahogany from Cuba, and boxwood from France. He starts with a beautiful piece of wood and makes a cut. The design begins to evolve, and the form emerges as he shapes the wood to enhance the richness of the wood figure.

Photo by Daniel Guilloux.

His work has a pleasant, tactile quality heightened by the contrast between sharp edges and smooth, highly polished curves. It is not surprising he has a blind client who enjoys his work by touch. Although he thinks of each piece as a sculpture rather than a functional object, most of his designs open as boxes with chiseled out drawers that pivot open on pins. By building complex drawers into his sculptures, he highlights the conversation among craftsmanship, art, and function. The drawers also encourage an interaction with the viewer. Although most of his creations are the size of small boxes, he has made pieces up to four feet in height that also contain drawers.

Couradin freely acknowledges the influence of the mid-twentieth century sculptors Constantin Brancusi and Henry Moore. He was inspired by Moore's metaphorical description of the tactile attraction of sculpture: "There is always something that lives under the skin of a piece of sculpture." In addition to the biomorphic, abstract shapes that characterize their work, Couradin shares their interest in nature and how the natural material shapes the art. Like them, he lets the grain of the wood dictate form.

Since 1990, Couradin has exhibited in galleries around France and beginning in 2001, galleries in England, Switzerland, Los Angeles, and Miami. His fervent hope is that his work will "arouse visual emotions that will lead to tactile pleasures."

Passion, 1997. Madagascan rosewood, various inlays; H. 39½" W. 19½" D. 15½". *Passion* was purchased by the town of Grenoble near where Couradin resides. An example of his "variable geometry," the piece is a smooth interplay of curves until a touch reveals angular parts that peel off to expose exotic inlays.

ANDREW CRAWFORD

Born: 1955, Dartford, Kent, England

Almost Anything Is Possible

Having a passion for both music and woodworking, Andrew Crawford might have been a musical instrument maker, but he likes the freedom of expression boxes offer. He enjoyed building plastic models as a child, and a high school aptitude test identified "spatial abilities," suggesting he had a talent for making things. Once, he tried his hand at constructing a bass guitar in his father's do-it-yourself garage shop, and even attempted the impossible trick of converting a Victorian piano into a harpsichord.

Originally trained on the flute from age ten and then classical guitar at the Royal College of Music in

Crawford has made hexagonal and oval boxes but prefers rectangular ones with concave sides.

London, Crawford left school in 1976 to play bass guitar in a rock band called *64 Spoons*. Although the band broke up about 1980 (no recording contracts), Crawford continued to play with various jazz, rock, and classical groups. At the same time, he took some evening courses at the London College of Furniture (now London Guildhall University) and studied wind-instrument repair and guitar making while supporting himself as a bicycle messenger and taxi driver.

In 1986, when an antique restorer friend offered to share a workshop with him, he opened a musical

ABOVE

Andrew Crawford applies his standard French polish to a box.

OPPOSITE

Lava, 2008. H. 9" W. 16" D. 12". Oak, amboyna veneer, dyed sycamore veneer, ebony, birch plywood.

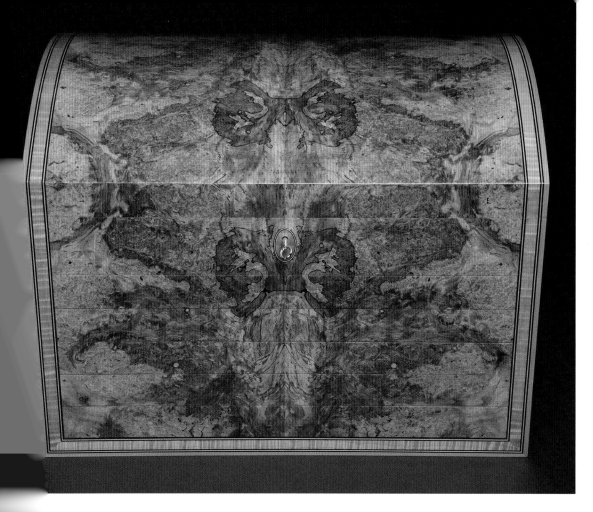

Cufflink Case, 2008. Elm, birch plywood, North American sweet gum burl, figured maple, lemon wood; H. 12" W. 18" D. 12". A single leaf of book-matched elm veneer decorates the front, back, and top of the box.

ABOVE

The maple banding is cut from solid figured maple blanks laminated between black-dyed and maple veneers. Sides and back feature a simple black/white/black band. Square lemonwood strips protect the exterior edges.

LEFT

Cufflink Case is fitted with five drawers. Each drawer has forty-eight compartments to accommodate cufflinks that come with their own boxes.

instrument restoration business. But he soon felt the urge to create, not just repair. Crawford built his first jewelry box in 1985 for a girlfriend on her twenty-first birthday. It had a domed lid and curved sides veneered with bird's-eye maple. The interior compartments were constructed of Cuban mahogany salvaged from an old table.

Hemmed in by large pieces of furniture in his shared garage-size shop, he decided to try making something smaller like a box. When his early boxes sold quickly, he phased out the musical instrument repair business. He labored in the London location until 2003, when he got married. The next year, he and his new wife moved to Shropshire, 200 miles northeast of London, where he now enjoys a shop with four times as much space.

Like several other box makers profiled in this book, Crawford believes his lack of formal cabinetmaking training allows him to take a fresh look at the field. He was also fortunate to have a parallel career as a flute player, so he could take his time making boxes. Although Crawford still plays professionally since moving to Shropshire, his box making, writing, and teaching have become his focus. He has written two books on box making and a third with fellow box maker, Peter Lloyd, to accompany an exhibition of boxes that toured the United Kingdom. He is working on yet another box-making book while running regular woodworking courses in his Shropshire workshop.

Crawford prefers rectangular boxes with concave sides and domed lids. The inspiration originally came from a pair of ship's decanters with wide bases that he remembers as a child. The sweeping curves on his boxes seem to rise like tree trunks from a tabletop. The curved sides along with diamond-shaped escutcheons done in mother-of-pearl or a contrasting wood have become standard elements of his jewelry boxes. Each box gets a French polish, even though it adds two or three extra weeks to the two to four months it takes to construct a fine box. The finish speaks quality and customers appreciate the extra effort required to build up the finish.

The boxes are fabricated with birch plywood or medium-density fiberboard (MDF) he shapes with a hollow plane, scrapes, and sands smooth. He miters the curved sides and joins them with blind splines. The domed lid is made up of two or three thin strips of birch placed over a form and glued. It is not the making of boxes per se that Crawford enjoys, but the decorating. The carcass serves as a ground for intricate inlay and veneer.

Always interested in a challenge, he once designed a box to store samples of cut and uncut lapis that has been mined in Afghanistan for 4,000 years. The brief called for the box to look 4,000 years old and well traveled. So, he veneered the box with Macassar ebony and then overlaid it with sections of wany yew burl to create the effect of worn and torn leather. The domed top opens to several stacked trays while the front side swings out to access three shallow drawers. The figured maple interior lined with gray velvet contrasts with the dark ebony and yew exterior.

The chest was the ancestor of *Treasure Island*, which he made in 1999. He first covered the plywood carcass with a blue-dyed veneer, and then laid more than forty pieces of amboyna over it. The irregular edges of the amboyna created the illusion

---

Although jewelry boxes are most popular, Crawford advertises that almost anything is possible. Because of his interest in the flute, Crawford is often called upon to make flute cases.

---

of a coastline on a map; complete with an X that marks the location of the treasure. Completing the treasure imagery, the chest was fitted with ebony straps suggesting an iron-covered strong box. The strips also hide the joints between the different pieces of veneer. The lid is attached with a piano hinge, and brass quadrant hinges stop opening at ninety degrees to avoid damage.

Lava follows in the *Treasure Island* tradition. Like *Treasure Island*, *Lava* was first veneered with sycamore-dyed claret and then overlaid with more than fifty pieces of striking extra-thick amboyna veneer, creating a complex pattern over the box, all united by ebony straps. The nail heads and hinges, the same width as the straps, are also made of ebony. In addition to the typical, claret-covered heartwood and honey-colored sapwood, this amboyna showed unusual grey, stone-like textures perhaps caused by mineral staining. The colors, shapes (complete with holes), and untrimmed, natural edges could only mean one thing, said Crawford—lava. A tray lifts out to expose the claret-colored leather lining the interior.

Crawford's jewelry boxes are fitted with trays joined with miters and splines, while similar boxes designed as tea caddies have two separate containers flanking a space for a glass mixing bowl. His *Harlequin Tea Caddy* was inspired by Pablo Picasso's harlequin paintings based on the multicolored costumes of seventeenth century Italian jesters. While his first tea caddy was painted, subsequent boxes were covered with individually cut and colored diamond inlays separated by thin black strips.

On his cuff link boxes and others containing drawers, no pulls disturb the highly figured veneers that cover the case. Instead, drawers open by means of an ingenious pin system that Crawford adapted from similar locking mechanisms on nineteenth century boxes. A series of pins made of bicycle spokes are inserted into slots or holes drilled into the back wall of the box and extend down to a sloped brass plate attached to the back of the drawer. As the drawer is pushed closed the pin slips into a hole in the plate. Raising the turned knob frees the drawer, which pops open by means of springs attached to the back of the box.

Although jewelry boxes are most popular, Crawford advertises that almost anything is possible. With his interest in the flute, he is often called upon to make flute cases. Other commissions have included containers to hold chess sets, playing cards, squash balls for a tournament prize, computer discs, coins, ashes (both human and pet), and Chinese exercise balls. His writing boxes, often fitted with secret drawers, are patterned after the desk models popular

in the early nineteenth century. He sells presentation cases to corporations and memento boxes to individuals to display baby rattles, silver spoons, watches, and special wine corks. Because his great grandfather, Tom Rowden, was a well-known English watercolorist he takes great pride in making watercolor boxes fitted for pigments, palettes, brushes, and water jars.

From an early age, Crawford made music with the flute. Today, he spends more time making boxes, but his colorful and finely crafted creations sing as beautifully as musical notes.

Jewelry Box, 2006. Myrtle, maple, dyed veneers; H. 9" W. 13" D. 5". The multi-colored band that borders the lid and front of *Jewelry Box* is made from dyed veneers. These are laminated and stacked in the appropriate order to create a decorative plank, from which thin strips are cut. The chest contains two maple trays lined with dyed leather.

MICHAEL CULLEN

Born: 1958, Pocatello, Idaho

Unquenchable Need To Make

How many cabinetmakers produce fantasy furniture? At first glance *Elephant Chest* does not look very fanciful, but Michael Cullen originally named the chest *Dreaming of the Land Just Beyond Elephant Mountain*. When he told Bebe Johnson at the Pritam & Eames Gallery the story that he had found the chest in the land beyond Elephant Mountain, she told him to just call it *Elephant Chest*. For Cullen, the fantasy is what the chest will contain—rare documents, fine jewelry, or precious coins.

Actually, the idea for this box sprang from the carved mini-skirt on another fantasy piece called *Girl Cabinet*. The carving on *Elephant Chest* suggests the mountains he bikes past near his home in Sonoma County in Northern California. The green milk paint captures the green of the grass and oak trees on those mountains, while the yellow-orange top suggests the fields in the valleys.

As a teenager, Cullen often haunted Telegraph Avenue near the Berkeley campus, where hundreds of enterprising craftsmen daily hawked their wares.

Cullen textured the edge of the top with a gouge like a tiny ice cream scoop to contrast with his smooth carving. He got the idea from studying the carving of Samuel McIntire, who worked in Salem, Massachusetts, in the early nineteenth century. The carved feet suggest flowers.

Photo by Barbara Cullen

ABOVE

Star Table, 2006. Red gum eucalyptus. Dia. 6'. Cullen designed *Star Table* for the 2006 *Inspired by China* exhibition at the Peabody Essex Museum in Salem, Massachusetts. After seeing Chinese root furniture, Cullen wanted to celebrate the tree and its life. He textured the slightly dished top to suggest hammered copper so that light creates subtle patterns on the surface.

OPPOSITE

Elephant Chest, 2000. Mahogany, redwood burl; H. 12" W. 16" D. 10½".

Neptune Table, 2008.
Macassar ebony,
Ceylon satinwood;
H. 40" W. 44" D.10".
In 2003, Cullen was
commissioned to
create a series of six
small sculptural tables
for a long hall designed
to display some of the
client's paintings. The
only constraint was the
tables be natural wood
and uncarved, though
he snuck in some
shaping of the three
seaweed elements.
Salt-water aquariums
in the client's home
inspired *Neptune Table*.

ABOVE

Orange Box, 2007. Basswood, ebony; H. 6" W. 8"
D. 2½". *Orange Box*, Cullen's version of a band-sawn
box, is quick to make (in theory) and uses up some
perfectly good scrap wood. This design exhibits
the qualities of ceramic vessels that he admires—
curvature, delicateness, and a non-directional quality
of the material.

Even though most of Cullen's cabinetry
is technically complex, he prides himself on
designing his work to appear deceptively
simple. In contrast to the ornate, almost
Art Nouveau exterior joined by miters and
splines at the corners, the interior is lined
with unfinished redwood burl glued over
four plywood panels. The redwood adds
a visual as well as an olfactory surprise.
While the thick lid could conceal a secret
compartment, and he has often slipped
newspaper articles or invitations into sealed-
up voids to be discovered in the distant
future, this time he left the space empty.

Cullen's only other container with three-
dimensional carving is *Gnome Box*. Made

One day he was invited to dinner at a friend's house and needed a mallet to tenderize the meat. They set off to buy one, but ended up at Cullen's shop making one.

of redwood, it is one of the few pieces he has left unpainted. Most of his chests are ornamented with surface carving derived from nature, with names like *Red Leaf*, *Spring Rain*, *Harvest*, *Snowflake*, and *Cosmos*. Many of his tabletops are also covered with rhythmic, geometrical patterns. In his early work, Cullen carefully laid out the designs, but for the past decade, he has explored a looser approach that is evident in such pieces as *Blacktable* and *Fish-Ties*.

Cullen's carving technique further evolved after participating in a 2001 conference in Whangerei, New Zealand. There he met Lynol Grant, New Zealand's premier traditional Maori carver, who invited him to work at his studio. Grant advised Cullen to use a mallet to achieve more control than simply pushing carving chisels by hand.

Many cabinetmakers develop a recognizable style and merely refine it throughout their careers. Cullen's carved and painted chests are easily attributed to his hand, but starting with *Elephant Chest*, some of his work does not fit the mold. His tables, for instance, reveal his interest in sculpture. *The Lilies* table looks like three giant lilies intertwined, and the *Picasso* table is a nod to Cubism. With the *Mad Hatter* table, he experimented with multi-axis and multi-centered turning.

Where did all of this creativity come from? As a young man, Cullen was making

things in a space he rented next to his father's shop at the docks in Oakland, California, where his father built circuit boards for industry. Both his grandfather and great-grandfather worked as cabinetmakers for the Southern Pacific Railroad. In a vivid childhood memory, Cullen recalls his grandfather showing him how to make the mount for a rack of deer antlers.

Cullen's mother was from Wuerzberg, Germany, the home of famous medieval carver, Tilman Riemenschneider. Hearing about him growing up, Cullen finally got the chance to actually see his work on an eighth-grade trip to Europe. Awed by the German masters, Cullen bought his first set of gouges and started carving wooden belt buckles.

The Lilies, 2005
Bubinga; H. 32" W. 32" D. 10". The idea for *The Lilies* was to create something sculptural that mimicked the curves of plants with large leaves. The top is carved from a single plank of bubinga, and each leaf is slightly dished to hold objects liked a cupped hand.

Photos by Don Russel.

Pisces Tables, 2007. Mahogany; H. 16" W. 46" D. 30 ½". Although more organic than his *Puzzle Table*, the *Pisces Tables* still can be rearranged to suit. As the name suggests, the idea for the tables came from the image of two seals gliding by each other.

As a teenager, Cullen often haunted Telegraph Avenue near the Berkeley campus, where hundreds of enterprising craftsmen daily hawked their wares. They showed him people could make most anything and earn a living at it. School shop classes reinforced his craft aspirations. The seed of a maker was planted, but Cullen's parents nudged him in a different direction.

In 1983, he earned a degree in mechanical engineering, but even then, he found time to take many studio drawing, watercolor, and sculpture courses. After graduation, Cullen worked as an engineer, but he longed to make, not just design. One day, while having lunch in the country, he looked over at a barn with a glass-enclosed breezeway. Two men were trying to catch a bird that was trapped in the enclosure. Cullen saw this as a metaphor for his own situation, and decided to quit engineering.

For the next few years, he tried a number of different jobs trying to make the transition to doing art as a profession. He started his own greeting card company, led bicycle tours, and took courses toward a teaching certificate. At some point, he perused the books by James Krenov, and read *Fine Woodworking* magazine. But the real turning point came after seeing photos of carved furniture by Judy McKie, and sculptural clocks by Wendell Castle. He finally realized he could combine his interest in art with his engineering background and make a living as an artist.

A lack of technical skills constrained what he could do. So, in 1986, Cullen enrolled in the Leeds Design Workshop run by David Powell in Easthampton, Massachusetts. Powell, a graduate of the Edward Barnsley Workshop and the Royal College of Art in England, emphasized traditional cabinetmaking techniques in his two-year curriculum. After completing the program, Cullen worked with furniture maker Jamie Robertson in the famous Emily Street workshop cooperative in Boston. In contrast to his traditional training at Leeds,

Robertson exposed him to contemporary methods of sophisticated veneering.

After a few years, he decided to move back to California. He rented shops in downtown Petaluma for sixteen years before moving, about four years ago, to his current location in the country. Although Petaluma is home to a number of wood artists, Cullen wanted to work surrounded by nature. His new shop, in a converted egg-sorting plant an easy bicycle commute from home, has twice the space of the old shop. Currently, he is training his fifth apprentice, Trevor Hadden, in much the way he was trained at Leeds. The program is part of the San Rafael-based Baulines Craft Guild, of which he is president.

Steeped in the structured program at Leeds and the precision work demanded at Emily Street, Cullen found the looser culture of the West Coast refreshing. This is reflected in his unusual *Elemental* series of benches made of recycled wooden railroad trestles, redwood tree roots, or other massive timbers. The series recalls the formidable, natural wood sculptures of J. B. Blunk, who resided in nearby Inverness.

Making is in Cullen's blood. One day he was invited to dinner at a friend's house. They were having abalone but needed a mallet to tenderize the meat. They set off to buy one, but they ended up at Cullen's shop making one. Cullen has an unquenchable need to make things, whether furniture, sculpture, boxes, or tenderizing mallets. In the making he makes magic, and his work becomes play. It is then that he is the happiest—and so are his customers.

Photo by George Post.

LEFT

Mad Hatter, 2004. Wood with silver cup; H. 24" Dia. 12". For *Mad Hatter*, a one-teacup table, Cullen collaborated with metalworking friend, Laurie Marson.

BELOW

Quintet with Cracked Ice (aka *Puzzle Tables*), 2006. Mahogany; H. 22" W. 42" D. 42". Made for the 2006 *Inspired by China* exhibition, these five tables can be arranged in many different ways. The carved, cracked ice motif on their tops refracts light in dramatic ways.

JENNA GOLDBERG

Born: 1968, Brewster, New York

Creating Boxes with Surprises

Jenna Goldberg is a cabinetmaker, a maker of large rectilinear cabinets that she uses as canvases to display a colorful vocabulary of carved and painted patterns. *Falling Leaves*, for example, a cabinet in the Smithsonian's Renwick Gallery collection, features intaglio carving of stylized leaves on the outside and rubber-stamped cranes

---

Completing commissions, filling requests for auction pieces, or making them just for fun, Goldberg has turned out more than a hundred boxes including square and curved ones and some with two and three trays inside.

---

on the inside. Another surprise is the vertical slats that cover the back, where a solid piece of plywood would be expected. They suggest the typical bead-board walls of a Victorian cottage. The exterior of her *Gingko Buffet* is covered with ginkgo leaves, while blowups of animals from Japanese matchbox covers decorate the interior.

Goldberg first heard about matchbox covers from a friend whose father had collected Japanese examples from the early twentieth century. When she began to look for them herself, she found collectors on e-Bay avidly sought them. Hooked, she began buying some herself. The motifs mostly depict animals such as elephants, birds, and lions, but sometimes include people, buildings, and crazy-looking airplanes.

Goldberg started making boxes about five years ago while on a retreat at the Haystack Mountain School of

All photos by Mark Johnston.

ABOVE

Jenna Goldberg in her studio.

OPPOSITE

Boxes, 2008. Basswood with Xerox transfers.
Blue: H. 4" W. 24" D. 5".
Red: H. 4" W. 19" D. 4".
Green: H. 4" W. 11" D. 5".

Gingko Buffet, 2005. Maple, cherry; H. 38" W. 60" D. 22". The gingko leaves, which she remembers from her time in Philadelphia, are accentuated by freehand carving and give no hint of the surprise that lies inside. Behind the door in the cabinet are blowups of traditional Japanese woodblock prints of landscapes, reproduced from matchboxes.

Crafts in Deer Isle, Maine. She discovered the instant gratification they offer, in comparison to cabinets, which can take several months to complete. Unlike the straight lines of her cabinets, boxes can become any shape she imagines and are not constrained by the strong and precise joinery of larger furniture. Completing commissions, filling requests for auction pieces, or making them just for fun, Goldberg has turned out more than a hundred boxes including square and curved ones and some with two and three trays inside. Once, she made a box for sixteen harmonicas, decorating the inside with transfer prints of Blues album covers.

It took some experimentation to figure out the proper way to cut and assemble her band-sawn containers. Starting with a block of wood, Goldberg cuts off the top

Originally trained as an illustrator, Goldberg uses carving to emphasize surface patterns, just as she used a pencil to highlight drawings. While she usually has a general idea of the look she wants, she aims for a gestural, free form quality.

and bottom, then saws out the sides and end pieces. Next, she saws a sliver, which will become the bottom part of the lid, from what remains of the original block. At

this point, she can finish the inside faces, being careful to leave the glue surfaces untouched. After the box has been glued together, the sawn sliver is propped up inside the box so that the top part of the lid can be glued onto it. The top piece is then trimmed to conform to the shape of the box body. Finally, she cuts and finishes the box handles. Goldberg makes it sound so simple, but if the components are not sawn and finished in the correct order, the project does not have a happy ending.

Although many craftsmen make band-sawn boxes, it is the carved and painted decoration that sets Goldberg's boxes apart. She learned carving from Kristina Madsen, who is known for delicate lace-like furniture decoration.

Originally trained as an illustrator, Goldberg uses carving to emphasize surface patterns, just as she used a pencil to highlight drawings. While she usually has a general idea of the look she wants, she aims for a gestural, free-form quality.

Goldberg attributes her interest in patterns to her high school years in Israel, where she was exposed to the repetitious patterns of Islamic art. She found the abstract mosaics and tiles of Muslim mosques and holy sites mesmerizing, ethereal, and meditative. Her interest is

Bobby H Wall Cabinet, 2004. Basswood; H. 56" W. 22" D. 14". The outside of *Bobby H Wall Cabinet* is an amalgamation of abstract forms from art and design books. The interior features rubber-stamped birds. Goldberg would never want them as pets but likes their shapes and the idea that they are mysterious.

Rose Vanity, 2007
Mahogany; H. 36"
W. 72" D. 24". The
outside of this vanity
is covered with stylized
leaves and roses while
interior compartments
have animals from her
Japanese matchbox
collection. The drawers
are band sawn.

in pattern, whether found on Antonio
Gaudi's cathedral in Barcelona, the Moorish
architecture of the Alhambra in Spain, the
chaotic and colorful decoration of Hindu
architecture in India, or the more controlled
compositions of nineteenth century
Japanese prints.

Goldberg also finds inspiration in graphic
shapes and textile designs. The blue pattern
on her largest box in the exhibit suggests
batik. Her favorite of the three boxes in the
exhibit is marked with the asterisk-shaped
handle, a motif she once saw imprinted on
the side of a cabinet.

But there is more. Goldberg says that
her cabinets as well as her boxes are like

people—different on the inside than on the
outside. While the largest box in the exhibit
has dividers sized to hold tea bags, the
exteriors of the other two give no hint of
the irregularly shaped partitions inside.

More surprises await. The insides are
embellished with transfer prints from Indian
matchboxes popular in the 1940s and 1950s.
While most of the images are of animals, the
blue box features an odd rendition of two
monkeys sitting together smoking. Goldberg
photocopies the images and then applies a
transfer gel that pulls the ink off the paper
and transfers it onto the wood.

Goldberg was born with the creative gene.
Both of her parents attended Rhode Island

School of Design, and they traveled the craft fair circuit in New England during the 1970s, selling his ceramics and her textiles. After a dozen years, the couple settled down to regular jobs, her father as a high school shop and art teacher and her mother as a cantor and bar mitzvah instructor.

Growing up, Goldberg was always making things. At one point, she aspired to be a shoe designer and made high heels out of tape and cardboard. Once she built and furnished a tree house. At age nine, her mother taught her how to use the sewing machine. Her repertoire included handbags, eyeglass cases, and skirts. She started with patterns for the skirts but never was good at following directions, always wanting to do her own designs. In her first commercial art venture, she sold painted and potato-printed T-shirts.

Goldberg became interested in making furniture at the University of the Arts in Philadelphia, where she took some courses from Michael Hurwitz, the noted studio furniture maker. After receiving her bachelor's degree in illustration there in 1990, she enrolled in the Genoa School in upstate New York, an offshoot of the Wendell Castle School that had just closed. After it too closed, she transferred to San Diego State University and found that Wendy Maruyama, the head of the furniture department there, was on sabbatical. When she heard rumors that that program also was endangered (it did survive) she transferred again, this time to Rhode Island School of Design where she worked with Rosanne Somerson and Alphonse Mattia, earning a master's degree in 1994.

Samba Cabinet, 2005. Walnut; H. 75" W. 23" D. 15". The radio was playing Samba music from Brazil when Goldberg was finishing this cabinet. Although walnut is a preferred wood for cabinetry, Goldberg found that it did not provide enough contrast with her paint. The exterior shows off Goldberg's typical abstract geometric forms while the interior is rubber-stamped. The slats in the back are set with gaps between them for air circulation.

After graduation, she settled in Ashville, North Carolina, but missed the museums, the fast pace, and the cosmopolitan atmosphere of the Northeast. In 2001, she returned to Providence, Rhode Island and set up her shop. That building was sold a year ago, so she moved to a new space in an old mill just north of Fall River, Massachusetts. Although she is the only woodworker in the cooperative, she enjoys the camaraderie of fifteen other artists in the building. Her colleagues must share the same astonishment that her clients experience when they lift the lids of her boxes or open the doors of her cabinets, and discover the exotic surprises waiting inside.

LOUISE HIBBERT

Born: 1972, Southampton, England

From Microbiology, High Art

Making a beetle, plankton, or a seedpod into a box is the excuse for Louise Hibbert to show the world wonders of nature that are too small for most people to appreciate. Even more than the surprising beauty of these creatures, Hibbert is inspired by the Darwinian way nature solves the problems of life and survival. Although she wants people to enjoy the beauty of these objects, her subliminal message is one of conservation and respect for our fragile natural environment.

Even as a child, Hibbert liked both biology and art. She was always making things, including her own clothes that she painted and dyed. Long before it became a fad,

Hibbert switched to sustainable native British woods, particularly sycamore, and her work turned to small-scale pieces with an organic appearance.

she got into trouble painting designs on her fingernails. But fate set her on the path to become an artist. Because she had demonstrated a talent for science, she intended to make that her career, but before applying to college, she spent a year completing an art foundation course. When she applied for admission to college, she was turned down for her first choice—a biology program—but she was accepted into the art program at the University of Brighton. In 1994, she earned a degree with honors in three-dimensional design, specializing in wood and plastics.

ABOVE

Louise Hibbert works at her Wadkin Burgreen lathe.

OPPOSITE

Coleoptera Pill Box, 2009. African blackwood, English sycamore, copper, stainless steel, pine, resin; H. 2¾" W. 5" D. 2".

ABOVE

Cinachyra Box, 2000. English sycamore, boxwood, acrylic texture paste, polyester resin; Dia. 4". Typical of her early work, the idea for *Cinachyra Box* started as a golf-ball sponge found in the Western Pacific but represents an amalgamation of many different sea creatures. Hibbert created the interior from an illustration of a radiolarian by Ernst Haeckel.

ABOVE RIGHT

Rhodanthe Box, 2004. English sycamore, silver gold, texture paste; H. 3½". Hibbert picked up a rhodanthe seedpod in Perth, Australia. She wanted to capture its subtle coloring in *Rhodanthe Box*.

Immediately after graduation, Hibbert took up woodturning professionally, working from a shop in Brighton and then in North Wales. She began making small laminated items like pens, jewelry, and boxes using exotic woods. She soon discovered the woods were not from sustainable sources, nor did she really enjoy the tedious lamination process.

Hibbert switched to sustainable native British woods, particularly sycamore, and her work turned to small-scale pieces with an organic appearance. She prefers to make diminutive pieces because people can pick them up, interact with them, and appreciate the exquisite detail. But more importantly, she can finish the piece before getting bored. Although she continues to do some production work like salt and pepper mills and bottle stoppers, more and more of her time is devoted to one-off challenges.

Although a turner by training, Hibbert says the lathe scares her. If she could bring her designs to fruition any other way, she would, but the lathe is the perfect tool for creating nature's symmetry.

Hibbert draws her inspiration from the natural world whether in a book, an aquarium, a botanical garden, or a museum. She is always looking at European scientific illustrations from earlier centuries, particularly the work of Ernest Haeckel where she first discovered the single-cell radiolarian she has featured in her work.

It is developing the idea, and the final airbrushing and texturing, that she finds most creative. Hibbert draws her inspiration from the natural world whether in a book, an aquarium, a botanical garden, or a museum. Rather than woods

with rich figure, she favors English sycamore because of its pale, even grain "that when colored glows with an intense vibrancy." She is always looking at European scientific illustrations from earlier centuries, particularly the work of Ernest Haeckel, where she first discovered the single-cell radiolarian she has featured in her work. His *Art Forms in Nature* influenced Art Nouveau designers at the end of the nineteenth century, and continues to stir artists today.

A turning point in Hibbert's career occurred in 2001 when she began working with Sarah Parker-Eaton, a jeweler whom she met at a crafts fair in London. Their collaboration has pushed her to greater creativity and technical skill. One of their first joint projects, a series of plankton forms, merged her love of biology with her art. Growing up on the ocean, Hibbert was always fascinated with marine life. Brightly

colored tropical fish swimming in the tanks at the local fish store mesmerize her. Plankton inspired much of her final student show at the university.

David Thomas, an oceanographer at the University of Wales, invited Hibbert and Parker-Eaton to his laboratory to watch these almost invisible sea creatures through electron microscopes. The result was a series of boxes and vessels based on what they saw in the lab, including *Radiolaria*, with a sycamore body and silver spikes, and *Corythodinium*, with a silver trimmed lid. They hoped their work would raise awareness of the vast amount of life teeming in the oceans that most people never see. In 2003, the two began a series based on jellyfish.

More recently, Hibbert and Parker-Eaton turned to the plant world for a project called *Genus Australis* that focused on seedpods and plants native to Western Australia. During a month-long residency

Haeckel Pod Box, 2008. English sycamore, silver, maple veneer, reclaimed leather, cotton thread; L. 5½". Before working in wood, Hibbert had focused on textiles. *Haeckel Pod Box*, with a ridged outer casing in leather and a soft lining to protect the inner pod, reminded her of horse chestnuts. Sarah Parker-Eaton fabricated the metal work.

in Perth, they visited a local seed bank and worked with FORM Gallery to draw attention to the unique native flora and the need to conserve them. *Pimpiniana*, for example, was inspired by the seedpod of the red flowering gum tree that dominates the Australian landscape, while *Thomasia* was based on the ovary produced by a local woodland shrub. In contrast to their smooth, brightly colored plankton pieces, the seedpod group featured earth tones and rough textures obtained by scorching and scratching the surface.

The idea for a bug box had been percolating since 2001 when Hibbert sketched a series of beetles but only made one. *Coleoptera* takes its name from the largest insect family, beetles, and its subcategory, weevils. They have long snouts and bulbous,

grooved elytra or external wings that protect the functional wings underneath. Instead of the scales usually found on this genus, Hibbert has given the insect antennae from (appropriately) the woodworm family of beetles.

Hibbert usually prefers to work with silver, but in this case, she chose copper to complement the beetle's emerald green body. She has textured the central section of the bug's body with pyrography to emphasize its armored exoskeleton. She turned the basic shape of the body before carving it, and then airbrushed the elytra with acrylic inks. A bit of gold dust made the green body iridescent. A fine inlay of patinated metal added additional detail. The bug conceals a stainless steel, airtight

Dinoflagellates Boxes I & II, 2000. I (left): English sycamore, ebony, acrylic ink, polyester resin, acrylic texture paste; L. 10½". II (right): English sycamore, yew, acrylic ink, polyester resin; L. 5". Landscape photographer Tom Carlise commissioned *Dinoflagellates Boxes I & II*. He wanted a plankton-inspired piece that provided both visual and tactile interest, and he specified the colors from a photograph he had taken in Nevada.

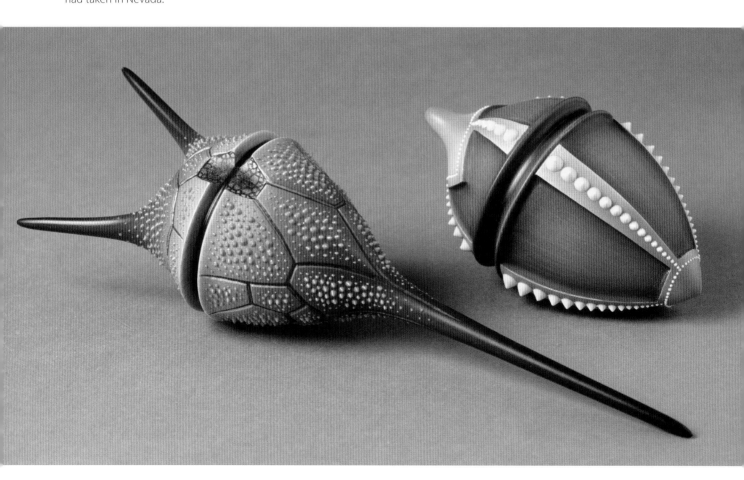

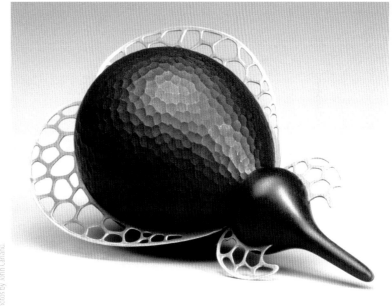

pillbox specifically designed to hold twenty-five nitroglycerin tablets.

After marrying Douglas Finkel, a turner and furniture maker who has taught at Virginia Commonwealth University, Hibbert moved to Gloucester, Virginia, in 2002. For the past three years, the couple has been building a log house and studio on a seven-acre wooded lot. Accustomed to working to precise tolerances, she has had to adapt to the looser fit of carpentry. While Hibbert misses the mountains and beaches of her native Wales, she enjoys the forests surrounding their new home and the nearby lake that teems with turtles, birds, and even a few eagles. Nature is her passion, and she wants her art to stir that same passion in the world.

Lace Bug Box, 2001. English sycamore, silver, African blackwood; L. 4½". The genesis of *Lace Bug Box* came from a glimpse of an image of a delicate lace bug in a museum bookshop. Hibbert made the box during an International Turning Exchange in Philadelphia. Mark Gardner, another artist and craftsman in the program, textured the body. When opened, *Lace Bug Box* highlights the silver Hibbert experimented with during the International Turning Exchange.

MICHAEL HOSALUK

Born: 1954, Ivermay, Canada

Work Expresses Inner Spirit

Michael Hosaluk always liked to make things. Growing up on a farm in western Canada, he started out creating slingshots and crossbows, which he once used to shoot out a high window in a grain elevator. His mother was always crocheting or knitting, and his father made furniture for the family. After high school, he studied cabinetmaking for a year in Saskatoon, Canada, and then

Hosaluk made more than a hundred skeleton chairs and other "containers" to stack in the gallery and scatter around the city, in acts of "chairorrism."

set up his own shop to make doors, windows, and just about anything else customers wanted. After about five years, it was either expand or quit to do what he wanted.

What he wanted to do was make something that was more important and more meaningful than mere house parts and commercial displays. The mid-1970s witnessed the debut of *Fine Woodworking* magazine and a growing interest in craft. Hosaluk saw the possibilities of making a living in that arena. He had been introduced to the lathe in high school and had practiced in his father's shop while reading all of the how-to books available. By 1981, he was confident enough to submit two objects to the Wood Turning Center in Philadelphia for an exhibition, and both were accepted. Also that year, he attended the last of the woodturning symposiums organized by the center.

ABOVE

Michael Hosaluk demonstrates the turning of a large disk at Arrowmont School of Arts & Crafts in Gatlinburg, Tennessee. He relishes his time teaching art camps for big kids where he can experiment and move in new directions. For him, teaching is learning.

OPPOSITE

Relationships, 2005. Australian jara, Canadian maple; H. 7" W. 10" D. 4".

Chair Lock in Oakland, California, 2006. Poplar, steel gate. This was one of the early acts of "chairorrism" that swept North America in 2006 and 2007 in conjunction with Hosaluk's exhibit at the Mendel Art Gallery in Saskatoon, Canada. The 100 chairs in the exhibit could be moved by anyone who entered the show. Others were scattered around town and elsewhere.

From the beginning, Hosaluk always believed in the benefits of exchanging ideas. To further educate himself he enticed illustrious turners such as Del Stubbs, David Ellsworth, and Mark Sfirri to come to Saskatoon to teach or to attend conferences that he organized beginning in 1982. He became the driving force behind the creation of the now world-renowned Emma Lake Collaboration in 1994.

Originally, the remote Emma Lake site had been set up as a summer retreat for artists in the 1930s. Hosaluk's biennial happenings attract turners and furniture makers from all over the world to meet and share ideas. Hosaluk and his crew haul all of the tools up to the lake to equip wood shops and more recently, studios for metal, glass, fiber, and other media. For the next biennial, he is thinking of calling it "Emma Unplugged," requiring participants to bring only the tools they can carry and then see what they can make with them.

Hosaluk's exposure to the burst of creativity that characterizes the Emma Lake phenomenon helps explain his own wellspring of creativity that he expresses in woodturning, furniture, and sculpture. Even before his involvement with Emma Lake, he fabricated a series of tables from aluminum, Colorcore, glass, and Plexiglas that was totally out-of-the-box for a wood turner. Called *Mach IV*, the three-legged tables with circular tops commemorated the birth of his fourth child. Ten years later, at the behest of his wife, Marilyn, he actually made several, more normal, four-legged tables out of birch and maple. He believes his strong grounding

LEFT

Yellow Cactus Chair, 2001. Maple; H. 46" W. 25" D. 22". Cactus would seem an uncomfortable material for a chair, but the seat is safe to sit on. As with most inspiration, the seed for the idea was buried in his subconscious. After he made *Yellow Cactus Chair*, Hosaluk remembered a drawing his three-year-old daughter had slipped into his tool cabinet a year earlier. The finished chair is very close to his daughter's design.

BELOW

Scribble, 2004. Maple with acrylic paint, ballpoint pen, charcoal decoration; H. 9" W. 8" D. 8". Doodling is a universal pastime. Hosaluk has decorated *Scribble* with somewhat frenetic designs.

in traditional woodworking has given him confidence for projects that are more creative.

Recently, Hosaluk had a one-man show at the Mendel Gallery in Saskatoon that explored the many meanings of the familiar chair. Taking his art in a radically new direction, he made more than a hundred skeleton chairs and other "containers" to stack in the gallery and even scatter around the city, in acts of "chairorrism." The idea was to make people think about this mundane object and what it says about humanity. An entirely different sculpture pokes out of the banks of the Saskatoon River in the form of abstract ship prows. Hosaluk enjoys the way people interact with these permanent additions to the park, which force them to consider the city's riparian heritage.

Similarly, the interactive quality of boxes is what attracts him. He has made all kinds of boxes from hope chests to small pocket-sized containers that men can carry in their pockets. *Relationships* are the final few in a series of maybe seventy-five groups he has constructed over the last ten years. Starting with an extra spout from an earlier collection of teapots decorated with enigmatic faces, Hosaluk turned cylinders and then cut them apart on an angle to glue them back together in a football shape. He then cut off the tips at an angle and again re-glued them, this

Summer Chest, 2002. Baltic plywood, maple; H. 36" W. 40" D. 18". *Summer Chest* displays Hosaluk's love of color and surface pattern. The decoration was inspired by Aboriginal art he had seen in Australia.

The exteriors of these two boxes are laboriously carved, burned, sanded, and carefully bleached, so that only the highlights are affected. The final finish looks rough but is actually quite smooth to the touch, just another surprise in the

Hosaluk has perfected the arts of the elegantly turned bowl and of beautifully crafted furniture, but what he is also known for is his richly decorated facades.

deceptively complex composition. It is also a surprise that the two pieces actually come apart to expose interiors with an entirely different texture. Although these containers are waiting to conceal some treasure, Hosaluk is thinking that his next series of boxes will include their own surprises.

Hosaluk has perfected the arts of the elegantly turned bowl and of beautifully crafted furniture, but what he is also known for is his richly decorated façades. He works intuitively to deposit evidence of his inner self and his personal history on the surface, much like a unique fingerprint or distinctive handwriting. In contrast to the first generation of turners, and indeed most early woodworkers whose emphasis was on technique and the beauty of the wood, Hosaluk uses wood as a vehicle to tell his own personal story. He sees the urge to decorate as primal. The decoration on his *Scribble* bowl, for example, represents personal doodles. A series of work with Ukrainian themes and motifs honors his cultural roots.

time in snail-like shapes. No two are the same shape or have the same surface.

The idea for the shape came from a walk on the beach where, always attuned to nature, he saw a similar curled form. Was it a sea slug, a shrimp, or some other ocean creature? He enjoys letting children interact with his pieces because they have such wild imaginations. He likes the work itself to speak directly to the viewer.

In *Relationships*, the pair of highly technical segmented turnings can be moved into any number of configurations to suggest the infinite complexity of human relationships. Opening in the middle, the boxes also can be put back together in different orientations. Indeed, one client told him that the couple positions the pieces as a daily barometer of their relationship.

In addition to these personal statements, the twin themes of interaction and relationships run throughout his oeuvre. He purposely participates in one local craft show a year, and routinely attends the annual SOFA exhibition in Chicago, primarily to get the reaction of people to his work.

For Hosaluk, his work is about revealing himself and who he is. He believes that everyone is born with an inner spirit and that this spirit, plus the life experiences of the artist, can be expressed in the work. The need to bare his soul as an artist is both exhilarating and liberating. He is master of materials and techniques, but more important is the content and what it evokes. Each project is an adventure, and Hosaluk never knows where his creative spirit will take him.

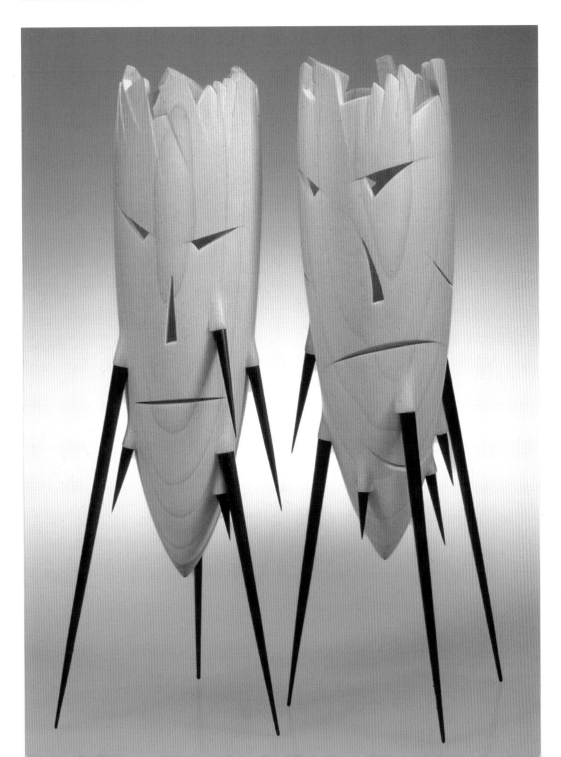

Introvert/Extrovert, 2000. Ash, blackwood; H. 12" W. 12" D. 5". These vessels are part of a series of self-portraits. Hosaluk observes that, "After a while, self-portraits are evident in all we do."

ROBERT INGHAM

Born: 1938, Delhi, India

Restrained Designs, Impeccable Craftsmanship

As principal of John Makepeace's School for Craftsmen in Wood at Parnham College, Robert Ingham trained many of the leading furniture craftsmen in Great Britain. Ingham emphasizes technique and is always pushing the limits of the craft. Drawing on a lifetime interest in engineering, he has developed special hand-operated machinery and jigs to produce some

---

Ingham began making boxes while teaching the first-year technique curriculum. He found that in a crowded shop, he could put aside a small box more easily than a large piece of furniture.

---

of the most technically complex boxes and furniture in the field. Indeed, he often refers to his work as "wood engineering."

Ingham decorated his first piece of furniture at the age of six. He had asked for an engineering set for Christmas, but in wartime Delhi where he was born, that was hard to come by. Instead, his father, an officer in the British colonial police, gave him a fretwork set. He was a bit disappointed until his father pointed out the shiny knife. He proceeded to carve up one of the family dining chairs.

After the partition of India and Pakistan in 1947, the Ingham family moved back to England to live in his father's family home in Yorkshire. In high school, engineering and woodworking teachers inspired Ingham

Photo by Imagephotographic

ABOVE

Robert Ingham works in his shop, checking the joinery of a box.

OPPOSITE

Treasure Chest, 2008. Macassar ebony, Swiss pear, American black walnut, ripple sycamore, abalone shell; H. 7¾" W. 16⅝" D. 9⅜".

Times 4, 2008. Bog oak, olive ash, walnut, abalone; H. 2" W. 9" D. 9". In *Times 4*, discs of abalone highlight each of the four separate lids.

to pursue a career in education. In 1961, he earned a teaching certificate with a specialty in silversmithing at Loughborough College, and a diploma with honors. He then taught for ten years in secondary schools while taking two years of additional training in furniture making at the City & Guilds of London Institute. Influenced by his brother, an industrial designer trained at the Royal College of Art, he enrolled in the Leeds College of Art to study design. Even though the degree could have led to a successful career in industrial design, Ingham had a passion for making. He also found high school teaching frustrating and limited by the rudimentary skills of the young students.

So, in 1971, he resolved to go into business with his brother. They opened a shop at Thirsk in North Yorkshire to make bespoke and limited-edition furniture. Five years later, his brother decided to open his

own workshop in Hemel Hempstead before moving to Australia to establish the furniture school at the Canberra School of Art.

In 1976, after a short stint in retailing and interior design, Ingham assisted John Makepeace, the renowned British furniture designer-maker, in setting up the School for Craftsmen in Wood at Parnham College in Dorset in the southwest of England. Under his tutelage, the two-year program literally spawned the profession of studio furniture making in England. Some of his students have helped train members of the American studio furniture movement, which in the 1970s was in its infancy. Although new graduates faced an uncertain future in the new profession, most felt it was a risk worth taking to satisfy their need for self-expression. Up to that time, most university programs separated design from making. Ingham and Makepeace firmly believed both were equally important.

Ingham began making boxes while teaching the first-year technique curriculum. He found that when teaching in a crowded shop he could put aside a small box more easily than a large piece of furniture. In

The designs of Ingham's boxes are generally restrained and his craftsmanship is impeccable.

fact, in the second year of the program, he introduced a student project to make a box with swiveling drawers. Stacked one above the other, the drawers swung open on pins much like the drawers in the Po Shun Leong box. He continues to use the technique on jewelry boxes including his *Jewelry Tower* and *Elaine's Treasure Chest*. He has adapted the same method for larger cabinets. But unlike Leong's drawers, which are cut out on a band saw, Ingham's drawers are all finely crafted with dovetail and mortise-and-tenon joints.

After twenty years at Parnham, Ingham decided it was time to get back to his own work full time. In 1997, he left the school and relocated to Bwlch Isa in North Wales near the mountains of Snowdonia. He works every day in a neat, 900-square foot shop he built into the hillside garden behind his house. Andrea, his wife of twenty-five years, manages the business end of the

Trio,1999. Purpleheart, bird's-eye maple; H. 2" W. 5" D. 12". When the lids of *Trio* are lifted, it is hard not to imagine the purpleheart insets as bright red smiling lips.

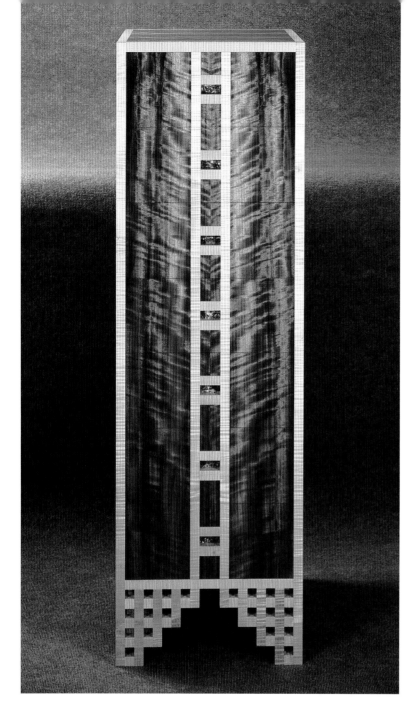

Lattice Tower, 2004. Silky oak, ripple sycamore with walnut, abalone inlay; H. 48" W. 16" D. 16". The inlaid squares on the front of *Lattice Tower* recall the work of Josef Hoffmann and the Vienna Secessionists of the early twentieth century, while the latticework that forms the feet are a nod to oriental design.

down version of his narrow *Lattice Tower* cabinet from 2004 that shows the influence of Japanese lattice construction.

Although the ebony and Swiss pear wood used in *Treasure Chest* create a striking contrast, he further captures the eye with inlaid abalone shell at the corners on the lid. It is a technique he employs frequently, selecting natural materials such as mother-of-pearl and cut stones to energize the eye. Ingham has carefully matched the grain pattern of the ebony and pear on both the outside and inside, to give the appearance that he has used solid woods. In reality, the woods are glued to a medium-density fiberboard (MDF) core. The MDF provides a stable ground, and besides, the ebony is only available as a veneer. The black walnut dividers in the two tiers of ripple sycamore trays mirror the exterior pattern.

The designs of Ingham's boxes are generally restrained, and his craftsmanship is impeccable. Drawing on his interest in engineering, he has adapted a metal milling machine to make the precision cuts necessary to fashion the three semicircular wooden butt hinges, the two stops (like the hinges but with a forty-five-degree bevel on opposing edges) and the large circle of pear wood on the lid. Obsessed with handcraftsmanship, he eschews any store-bought hardware and has even fabricated the brass spring lock. The audible click of his handmade lock when it closes adds an audible dimension to the visual pleasure.

While pursuing his own woodworking career, Ingham has continued to advocate for the integration of design and making both in his recent book, *Cutting Edge*

enterprise. Trained as a graphic designer, she also provides invaluable aesthetic advice and helps solve design problems. Looking out every day on the Welsh mountains that inspire him, Ingham divides his work about equally between boxes and furniture.

Ingham has always liked containers, and sometimes his furniture resembles scaled-up boxes while other times the reverse. *Treasure Chest* (named by his wife, who thought the jewelry box looked like one) is a scaled-

Cabinetmaking, and in articles in the British magazine *Furniture and Cabinetmaking*. For five years, he served on the research and advisory board of Buckinghamshire Chilterns University College in High Wycombe, north of London, which was the center of the British furniture industry in the twentieth century. Traditionally concentrating on furniture design, the college wanted better integration of technical aspects and design.

Ten Guild Marks awarded to his furniture by the Worshipful Company of Furniture Makers have recognized Ingham's extraordinary craftsmanship. He was invited to join the Worshipful Company of Furniture Makers, honored with a grant of Freedom of the City of London, and was made a Fellow of the Society of Designer Craftsmen. Until recently, he taught regularly in Great Britain and the United States and showed at Pritam & Eames Gallery on Long Island.

ABOVE

Nave Altar, 2006. Bleached oak, fumed oak, plate glass; H. 36" W. 78" D. 36". The Dean of St. Asaph Cathedral in North Wales commissioned *Nave Altar* in order to have contemporary art in this fourteenth century cathedral.

LEFT

Hobson's Choice, 2001. Bird's-eye maple with walnut and abalone inlay; H. 30" W. 48" D. 16". *Hobson's Choice* is the hall table Mr. and Mrs. Hobson commissioned to hold their telephone, with drawers for directories and a cupboard below to house the children's shoes.

RAY JONES

Born: 1955, Ukiah, California

Boxes Engineered for Beauty

Now a full-time woodworker, Ray Jones originally studied aeronautical engineering. During the summer months, he worked for a builder in his hometown of Healdsburg in northern California. There, he had the good fortune to work for a man who believed (a) in doing things right rather than quickly and (b) that he could make almost anything he needed. The experience

---

One of Jones' early products was a round postage-stamp-holder about the size of a billiard ball with a flat bottom.

---

gave Jones confidence to work with his hands. So, after graduating from college and moving to Los Angeles to begin his new job developing ramjet engines, he bought tools instead of furniture and made what he needed to furnish his first home.

Later, Jones tried his hand at making gifts, and in 1981, designed a jewelry box for his future wife, Linda. The rectangular container featured wooden hinges and rounded front and back sides. The design, now available in nine sizes and a choice of woods, became a staple of his business after he left engineering in 1982 to embark on a new woodworking career. He loved engineering but did not like working on military programs, the nine-to-five regimen, nor living in a big city. Jones produced wall clocks, rolling pins, letter openers, bud vases, and other small items he sold at craft fairs and galleries. He eventually concentrated on boxes, as they interested

Photo by Linda Hylson.

ABOVE
Ray Jones works on an *Omega* box in his shop during 2008.

OPPOSITE AND BELOW
Omega V, 2008. Mahogany, pommele bosse, ebony; H. 19" W. 18" D. 8".

him the most and sold well. In 1990, he moved to Asheville, in the mountains of North Carolina, where he continues to work fourteen-hour days in his garage studio.

One of Jones' early products was a round postage-stamp-holder about the size of a billiard ball with a flat bottom. While turning them by the hundreds, his mind was busy designing a spherical box. Although most turned boxes have lift-off lids, he wanted to make ones with hinged lids or doors. These musings eventually resulted in his *Hidden Treasure* series of boxes shaped like slightly flattened spheres about the size of volleyballs. He turned the first ones from Baltic birch plywood because he wanted a stable material. He made the boxes with four doors and circular trays attached to each door. A variation, which he called *Hatch Box*, opened from the top like a gull-winged car.

He had been using traditional butt hinges but made them out of wood. After reading an article in *Fine Woodworking*, he eliminated the plates and now uses only the cylinders. He turns them out of ebony because of its strength and its uniform grain. The barrels are cut into three sections: two are glued to the box, and one to the door. They rotate on wooden pins topped with turned finials. He likes the interplay of cylinders with curved surfaces.

Although the Baltic birch plywood worked for the *Hidden Treasure* series, it had limitations. The plywood adhesive was abrasive, quickly dulling his turning tools. Moreover, the material came in only one very light color, and small defects routinely showed up in the most visible places. Jones began to make his own plywood by gluing up layers of veneer. And by varying the

Faithful Friend, 2006. Tasmanian blackwood, plywood, ebony, madrone burl; H. 15" W. 15" D. 8". Designed as a pet cremation urn, the madrone burl vessel, fitted with an ebony stopper on the front, lifts out. A turned pedestal allows *Faithful Friend* to stand with the opening up so that it can be filled.

Each door of *Fledgling* has a madrone burl shelf attached to the inside. The fifth shelf in the middle is stationary.

ABOVE TOP

Fledgling, 2000. Avodire plywood, madrone burl, ebony; H. 8" Dia. 13".
Fledgling is a variation of his *Hidden Treasure* series. The ebony column in the front is a latch, with a pin that must be raised to open. The other two ebony columns serve as hinges.

wood species, he could produce his own
defect-free plywood in any number of
colors. He makes his favorite plywoods from
avodire, mahogany, walnut, and okoume.

In the mid-1990s, Jones designed another
turned box that took a very different
approach from *Hidden Treasure*. First, he
turned a large bowl-shape from a solid
wood blank, cut the bowl in half, and glued
the two halves together rim to rim. He then
flattened one end to make a base, so the
box could stand vertically. Although most
of his boxes are fitted with trays, these have
oval-shaped drawers, made of aromatic
Spanish cedar, that run on dovetail-shaped
slides. Jones saws the drawer fronts from
a solid blank previously shaped to match
the contour of the box body. The standing,
semicircular silhouette gave the series its
name—*Halfmoon*.

Soon after moving to Asheville, Jones
joined the Southern Highlands Craft Guild,
which is headquartered there. The 1999
theme for the guild's annual exhibit was
Closures. This inspired him to design a box to
hold a pair of knives made by a friend who
had recently died. *Tribute to a Friend* consisted
of two twelve-inch-diameter saucer shapes
turned from spalted madrone burl and glued
together. The two doors open to reveal the
knives mounted inside like crossed swords.

This box evolved into his *Omega* series,
which he considers to be among his most
successful designs. It consists of two
eighteen-inch-diameter flattened bowl
shapes turned from handmade plywood and
mounted vertically. An arched cutout joins
a bent-laminated arc to form a base. The
outline of this circle above an arc recalls the

Greek letter omega, hence the name of the series. Jones was so happy with the design that he originally called it the *Bull's Eye* series, partly for the concentric circles, but mostly because he thought the design hit the target.

The front bowl is cut in half vertically to form doors. They swing open to reveal twelve oval-shaped trays. Four of them, each

---

Driven by a love of wood throughout his career, Jones constantly searches out exotic woods with unusual figures, colors, or textures.

---

spanning the width of the box, are attached to the back wall, with four smaller trays secured to the inside of each door. The light wood of the trays contrasts nicely with the plywood body. To make the trays, Jones saws nested ovals from a solid block of wood and then glues on quarter-inch-thick bottoms. The bottoms extends past the back of the trays to form curved tenons. The tenons fit into a matching slot in the inner wall of the box. The trays hang securely in place, and lift out easily.

Driven by a love of wood throughout his career, Jones constantly searches out exotic woods with unusual figures, colors, or textures and has used more than sixty different species from all over the world. He is particularly interested in salvaged, plantation grown, or harvested wood from sustainable natural forests. Among his favorites are black mangrove, spalted strangler fig, and Indian rosewood, a non-native tree that many years ago was introduced into Florida. Using no stains or dyes, he finishes the boxes with a mixture of

polyurethane, linseed oil, and mineral spirits to produce a silky smooth finish. As he says, "Nature has provided a wonderful palette. How can I improve upon that?"

In the late-1990s, Jones was asked to design a box to hold a plaque honoring Tetsuya Fujita, the American meteorologist who conceived the F scale for rating tornadoes. Recently, he was commissioned to make three sets of ping pong paddles and their presentation cases for President George W. Bush. The president gave one to Kosovo's head of state during an official visit to the White House, and the other two to the leaders of China during the 2008 Olympics. Despite the pressure of a tight deadline, Jones is proud his boxes have played a small role in international diplomacy.

Production Boxes, 2000. Top to bottom: avodire, spalted beech, chakte kok, mesquite, curly maple, myrtle burl, bird's-eye maple, Cuban mahogany. Smallest: H.1¾" W. 3½" D. 4". Largest: H. 5" W. 15" D. 9". These production boxes have been Jones' staple for more than twenty-six years. Each is made entirely of wood, including the hinges, fasteners, and all hardware. The design is based on a box he made for his future wife in 1981.

KIM KELZER

Born: 1957, El Paso, Texas

Pop Culture Becomes Fine Art

Kim Kelzer made *Hi/Lo* in Mark Bishop's studio in Stanley, during a three-month stint in Australia. Bishop had invited her and her boyfriend, Mike Scott, a turner, to participate in a show at his Stanley Art Works gallery. In the month before the show, Kelzer made about a dozen boxes and other small items. One constraint was

---

In the early 1990s, before she began making band-sawn boxes, Kelzer experimented with complex containers.

---

that the band saw was Bishop's only working machine. It was not a problem because Kelzer likes to have parameters that simplify her choices while at the same time adding to the challenge.

The boxes included several irons in different colors, a couple of wavy boxes, a square one, and one with handles made from an old towel bar. Handles on some of the others were formed from twisted wire. They reminded her of the metal insulation on antique cast-iron stove parts.

Kelzer sawed the bottom part of *Hi/Lo* out of a scrap of huon pine she found in Bishop's shop and shaped the top out of the wood cut from the interior. The lid of the box rests on a narrow lip cut from the blank while another slice forms the bottom, which she covered in red leather. She found the iron spike for the handle, the grommets, and other metal parts in a vacant lot behind the shop. She modified the little metal case, which came

ABOVE

Kim Kelzer in her studio. She has never understood why all machinery comes in battleship gray.

OPPOSITE

Hi/Lo (Red Iron Box), 2005. Huon pine, leather, found metal objects; H. 10" W. 12" D. 4½".

from an old heater or vacuum cleaner, by adding a black switch to give it the *Hi/Lo* name. After painting the inside and outside of the box, she oiled the whole thing with

---

Kelzer decorates her work with all manner of ornament including mosaics, pottery, and glass, always to make a point, a joke, or both.

---

something smelling of citrus that she found in the shop.

Almost all of Kelzer's work is painstakingly painted, but her Australian friends were horrified. Unbeknownst to her, Australians have a mystical reverence for Tasmanian huon pine which, along with the

bristlecone pine, is the longest-living tree in the world, some being as old as 4,000 years. Highly resistant to the toredo marine borer, the wood was over-harvested for boat building. To preserve the remaining trees, loggers salvage logs from swamps and rivers, and pull up old tree stumps. At least none of the rare wood in Bishop's shop went to waste. The chunk from which she cut her box had itself been a scrap from another project and in turn, her scrap became yet another smaller box.

In the early 1990s, before she began making band-sawn boxes, Kelzer experimented with complex containers such as *Toaster Coaster*. The series was inspired by her collection of 1950s appliances.

Banana Hammer, 2008. Wood, found metal hammerheads; H. 3" W. 11" D. 9". What could be more ridiculous than a *Banana Hammer*? A bunch of banana hammers.

Carved in basswood, this elegant box was a whimsical copy of a chrome-plated toaster on wheels with burnt toast popping out of it. Another container she called *Ripe* looked as if it were jammed into the top of a bright red tomato. Although both were carefully sculpted, the colored and textured surfaces were the focus.

Although primarily a furniture maker, Kelzer has created many smaller things over the years. She made a series of lamps using parts of 1950s irons, which she has collected for some time, and a series of similarly shaped boxes followed. After wrestling with big furniture, she likes to make small things as a break. Boxes and, sometimes, lamps are a welcome change of pace and provide a fast way to try out new forms, textures, and shapes. Instead of making a model that would sit uselessly in her shop, she could actually sell her experiments.

Everyone in Kelzer's family was handy. Her father once built an addition on their house and made the bar and bar stools to go in it. As the oldest child, she was the chief helper. At one point, she signed up for a woodshop class partly to twit her traditional father, but also because she knew where the boys were. She put herself through San Jose State University as a cake decorator and tailor, earning a degree in painting, and then went on to get her master's degree from the program in artisanry at Southeastern Massachusetts University. There, she worked with furniture makers Alphonse Mattia and the late Michael Pierschalla. Her thesis, on the influence of popular culture (television, cars, fabric, feminism, etc.) on furniture

Photo by Rachel Olsson.

Recreational Vehicle Liquor Cabinet, 2001. Wood, glass, found objects, steel; H. 53" W. 14" D. 12". Kelzer created *Recreational Vehicle Liquor Cabinet* for a show called *Recreation/Recreation* using recycled materials. Her cabinet revolves around drinking and watching television.

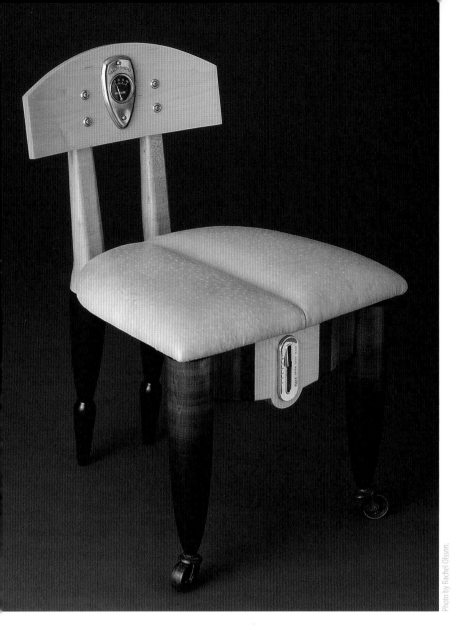

Photo by Rachel Olsson.

Lap Dance Chair, 2002. Wood, found objects; H. 31" W. 22" D. 19". *Lap Dance Chair* was probably not what the American Craft Museum had in mind when they put out a call for furniture about the body.

objects came from a dump located near her studio in Freeland, Washington.

An even more overtly feminist statement was *Lap Dance Chair*, which she made for a show about the body at the American Craft Museum. It started with a metal slot, part of a washing machine lint collector, that said "Clean Daily." She thought it looked rather vaginal. She lined it with pink fur and built the chair around it. The seat swivels on a lazy Susan mechanism, and a pressure gauge attracts the eye to the crest rail.

Over the past few years, Kelzer has become discouraged with the reluctance of customers to pay for the time required to make useful furniture that is both well-crafted and beautiful. People want cheap, disposable furniture that they can change every few years. She has come to believe that the public will pay a premium for essentially useless art but has little respect or appreciation for functional art objects.

Kelzer recently made a tentative foray into pure art with a series of oil-can sculptures. The oil-can assemblages, all carved in wood, are so realistic people think they are real. Early in her career, she used color to add texture and pattern to her work, but in this assemblage, the texture and pattern come from the variety of oil cans.

In the summer of 2008, Kelzer completed her final furniture commission and has embarked on a full-time career as a sculptor. Unfortunately, she is not the only studio furniture maker to leave the field to pursue a more lucrative livelihood in pure art.

A museum exhibit of non-functional, commemorative tools made to celebrate

design, has been a source of inspiration throughout her career.

Following the example of Judy McKie and other prominent women in the studio furniture movement, Kelzer has been making furniture since 1985. She decorates her work with all manner of ornament including mosaics, pottery, and glass, always to make a point, a joke, or both. Even her band saw is painted pink with white polka dots. For a cabinet called *Home on the Range* from 1991, she used painted wood, Plexiglas, neon tubing, and aluminum to parody a kitchen stove. Some of the found the opening of railroads and the dedication of bridges inspired her most recent body of work as a full-time sculptor. Her non-functional tools—flaccid or bloated hammers, a folding saw, and a giant garden spade—all represent nostalgia for an earlier, more craftsman-like era.

Some of her work has an edge. *Grave Diggers* consists of a pair of spades with bones for handles and skeleton-like faces cut into the shovels. A pair of hedge shears sports handles made to look like the blackberry cane that surrounds her house. A particularly striking sculpture features three intertwined hammers with handles made of yellow bananas, all carved in wood. She says the design came to her in a dream. All these ideas are conveyed in her characteristic funny, irreverent, and sarcastic way, a style that has marked her as one of the most creative makers in the field.

ABOVE

Grave Diggers, 2008. Wood, shovels; H. 24" W. 6". The bone handles and the macabre faces on the shovels in *Grave Diggers* leave no doubt about their intended use.

RIGHT

Railroad Cans, 2008. Painted wood; H. 3" to 36". Kelzer's early work used lots of color, texture, and pattern. In *Railroad Cans*, the pattern is in the variety of the oil cans, and the texture lies in their forms playing off one another.

STEVEN KENNARD

Born: 1956, Enfield, England

Boxes with Eternal Appeal

From the young age of twelve, Steven Kennard was influenced by a schoolteacher who saw his potential and encouraged his interest in woodworking. Kennard was always making things. His grandfather was a cabinetmaker and gave him tools, nurturing his growing creativity. After leaving school in the early 1970s, Kennard joined the legendary British music and theater group, *Magic Lantern*, and began fabricating stage sets and illusions. His first boxes contained women who were cut apart or cremated on stage, only to re-emerge unscathed at the end of the act.

He left the theater after a couple of years on the road and began restoring antiques, making reproductions, and producing custom furniture in Suffolk, England. The furniture often required turnings, mostly spindles.

Kennard left the theater after a couple of years on the road and began restoring antiques, making reproductions, and producing custom furniture in Suffolk, England.

He also began to make simple boxes and bowls that incorporated components from the furniture. He accepted commissions for architectural elements used in both new buildings and historic restorations, which frequently required lathe work. By the early 1980s, Kennard commenced to exhibit his turned work, including boxes, in Suffolk.

All photos by Steven Kennard.

ABOVE

Steven Kennard in his Canning, Nova Scotia, workshop.

OPPOSITE

Hat in a Box, 2005. Snakewood, African blackwood; H. 5¼" W. 2½" D. 2½".

In 1989, he moved to France and opened a studio in a 400-year old farmhouse in the Dordogne. During his time in France, he departed from traditional forms and began to experiment with surface decoration, which would become a signature of his later work. He credits Stephen Hogbin, the well-known Canadian turner and writer, for opening his eyes to the idea that turning could be sculptural.

As his work evolved, he began to exhibit it more widely in France. In 1990, well-known French sculptor Dominique Rayou, impressed with Kennard's artistic talent, included him in an exhibition at a gallery in Sarlat. A year later, he was chosen as one of three artists to represent the Aquitaine in an exhibition in Fukuoka, Japan.

In 1997, Kennard moved to Nova Scotia with his Canadian-born wife, Ellie. He opened a studio in Canning in the picturesque Annapolis Valley, which has a vibrant arts and crafts community. His shop is in a converted barn usually filled with music that both inspires him and aids his concentration. His turnings quickly found their way into collections worldwide including in Asia, Europe, Scandinavia, and North America.

Kennard continues to make boxes and furniture in addition to giving turning courses in his studio. He also works as a professional photographer, finding elements in his boxes that have been inspired by his pictures. The pattern on a box he called

Tread Softly, 2007. African blackwood, cocobolo, French boxwood; H. 2¼" Dia. 3". The surface of *Tread Softly* suggests stone pavers, and the name comes from a W. B. Yeats poem, "I have spread my dreams under your feet. Tread softly because you tread on my dreams." Kennard views his work as spreading his dreams under the feet of those who see it.

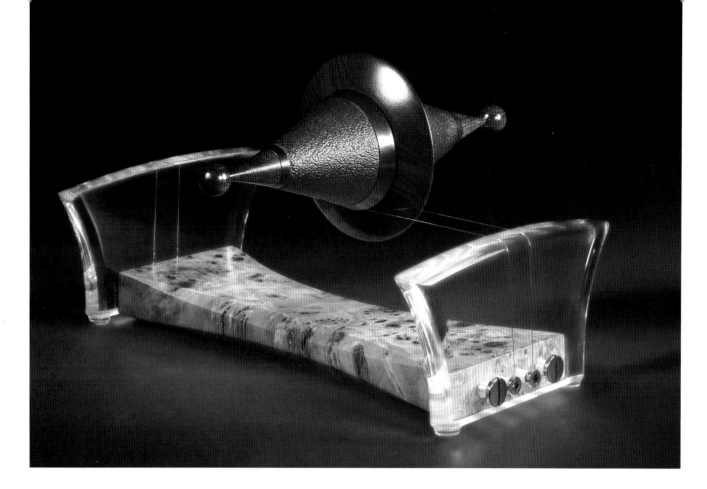

Tread Softly, for example, was inspired by his photographs of a cobbled street.

Kennard has been making boxes for thirty years, and many involve a turned hollow cone. This is surprising, since none of his earlier work in England or his early furniture takes that shape. He has used the cone in such boxes as *Big Top* that suggests a clown hat or a circus tent, in *Drop Box* to recall a raindrop falling into water, and in *Golfer's Dream* to conjure up a golf tee.

In designing *Saturn* in 1999, he realized that a box did not need to have a flat bottom. Instead, the turned, cone-shaped body is weighted so it rests upright on any surface. Since then he has made many variations such as *Maypole*, a similar shape but with multiple woods and textured, surface patterns.

Hat in a Box also has a cone-shaped body, but it is contained in a concave platform supported on cylindrical legs. Other versions such as *Tulip Ball* and *French Connection* sport ball feet in contrasting woods and turned convex platforms.

The cylindrical legs of *Hat in a Box* are fastened to the notched corners with two

---

Kennard continues to make boxes and furniture in addition to giving turning courses in his studio.

---

polished stainless-steel rods that hold them slightly off the square platform. The sides of the notches are shaped to follow the contours of the turned legs. Kennard turns most of his boxes by eye, but because the many different parts of this one had to fit snugly, he developed some special jigs.

Much of the appeal of his boxes lies in the surface decoration. He first experimented with decoration in France

Wired, 2005. African blackwood, cocobolo, poplar burl, Plexiglas, mother-of-pearl, steel guitar string; W. 8" Dia. 3". *Wired* evokes dreams of a tight ropewalker balancing above the bed.

French Connection,
2007. African
blackwood, French
boxwood; H. 6¼"
W. 4" D. 4". Deceptively
simple in appearance,
French Connection is in
fact the most refined
and difficult to make
of all the boxes in this
series. The Eiffel Tower
shape and the French
boxwood make the
French connection.

when he used watercolors to paint turned lamp bases and candlesticks. During the past decade, paint has given way to texture. In *Hat in a Box,* the smooth snakewood legs and bowl contrast with the textured African blackwood platform and cone-shaped lid. The smooth ball topping the cone contrasts with the textured cone and provides an inviting handle.

At first, Kennard used an engineer's punch, something like a miniature jackhammer, to work the surface. This was both tedious and shocking to his fragile turnings. Looking for a more efficient technique, he saw a friend's Foredom machine, which drives a cutter on a flexible shaft. Used mostly by jewelers and woodcarvers, this tool is like a versatile dental drill that can be fitted with different burrs, rasps, and cutters.

About a quarter of the time to make *Hat in a Box* was spent on texturing. On other boxes, texturing might require the same amount of time as turning the parts. Recently, Kennard has moved away from an overall sandblasted effect to designs that are more figurative. He suggests the look of brick or rustic stone on the cylindrical sides and top of his *Tower Box*. The serrated edges that encircle the body of *Soleil* recall a circular saw blade, while *Birthing Box* takes a more organic shape.

Nature is another important influence. One of his latest boxes, for example, has a row of etched apple trees in winter encircling the turned body. Called *Lost Orchard*, it pays homage to an apple orchard cut down near his house.

African blackwood is the perfect canvas for texturing. It is dense and stable, so delicate turnings are relatively strong, and it has little visible figure to distract from the surface pattern. A member of the rosewood family, blackwood was the wood of choice for traditional nineteenth century turners of wooden boxes. Now rare, it is used mostly to make wind instruments such as clarinets and bagpipes. He also likes the highly figured snakewood that is equally dense and contains natural oils that facilitate a fine finish.

Although Kennard has found it difficult to make a living solely as a woodturner, his boxes have an eternal appeal. One client used his *Saturn Box* to hold an engagement ring, while another stored a child's baby teeth in the box. Most, however, collect his boxes purely for their intrinsic aesthetic beauty, not as functional objects. Harkening back to his days making boxes for theatrical performances, Kennard continues to be fascinated by their mystery and the surprises they might contain.

Birthing Box, 1993. African blackwood, tagua nut; H. 5" Dia. 3¼". A metaphor for the creative process, *Birthing Box* represents pearls moving from the body up the birth canal to be born at the top and fall down into the concave base.

YUJI KUBO

Born: 1954, Hirosaki City, Japan

Experiments with Nontraditional Colors

During Commodore Matthew Perry's expedition that opened Japan to trade with the West in the 1850s, the two countries exchanged gifts. The American gifts included a small-scale train, while the Japanese gifts featured lacquer work. The West had been fascinated with oriental lacquer work since the seventeenth century, but no one knew the secret of how to make it. Japanning became a popular decoration on European and American furniture and other items, but it was a poor

---

As Kubo worked to master the old techniques, he wanted to do something different and break with tradition, to explore new patterns and new colors.

---

imitation. Unbeknownst to Perry, the wares he brought back to America were not the best quality.

In contrast, lacquer work by Yuji Kubo would be fit for an emperor. Except that they both produce a high gloss, Japanese lacquer has no relationship to the modern synthetic finish of that name. The basic material for oriental lacquer is the sap called urushi from the *Rhus verniciflua* tree. A member of the sumac family native to the Himalayas, the tree grows all over Southeast Asia. It takes about ten to fifteen years for the tree to mature, and after about a cup of sap has been harvested, the tree dies. The sap is then purified and aged for several years, much like wine.

ABOVE TOP
Yuji Kubo in his workshop.

ABOVE BOTTOM
Kubo's home and workshop on a mountainside surrounded by nature.

OPPOSITE
The Boat, 2007. Beech, urushi lacquer, gold leaf; H. 7¼" W. 25¼" D. 8¼".

Adding to the difficulty of working with lacquer is the fact that urushi contains the same irritant found in poison ivy. About half of the people who are exposed to it break out in an itchy rash. It is that same substance, however, that makes lacquer hard and durable. Japanese urushi is considered the highest quality, but the local product is so scarce that ninety percent of it is now imported, mostly from China.

The ancient art of lacquer work is practiced today throughout Japan in more than twenty locations, each with a different approach. Kubo resides in one

of those centers in Hirosaki City, in the northernmost prefecture on Japan's main island of Honshu, the farthest north that urushi is harvested. This agricultural region is the home of Tsugaru lacquer, the most sought-after type because of its smooth surfaces, rich colors, and dazzling patterns. Although archeological evidence indicates that lacquerware was used in Japan as early as 8000 B.C.E., the modern lacquer industry came from China mostly during the Tang Dynasty. Ruling China from the seventh to the tenth centuries, this dynasty presided over a golden age of Chinese culture. Lacquer work flourished in the Japanese imperial city of Edo, and gradually craftsmen migrated into the countryside to establish local manufactories. Since the lacquer-making tradition has virtually died out in China, Japanese lacquer today is recognized the world over for its beauty and durability.

Early in the seventeenth century, the Tsugaru clan, who extended their dominion over the Tohoku area, constructed Hirosaki Castle. The clan leaders encouraged lacquer craftsmen working in Edo to settle in the area. Under their patronage, the Tsugaru lacquer tradition was born. Initially, this lacquer was used to decorate swords and other weapons because it is stronger and more durable than any other lacquer. The government recognized Tsugaru as a traditional Japanese craft in 1975.

Kubo is following in that tradition. He was born in Hirosaki and returned there in 1976 after graduating from the University of Tokyo with a business administration degree. Unable to find work, he reluctantly

took a job in his father's lacquer workshop. As he worked to master the old techniques, he wanted to do something different and break with tradition to explore new patterns and new colors. In 1985, he opened his own studio and the next year participated in his first Tokyo exhibition, *New Lacquerware*. A year later, the Japan Ministry of International Trade and Industry honored him with its Good Design Award.

Kubo felt constrained by the eight traditional colors of Tsugaru lacquerware. He soon became known for experiments with nontraditional colors. Although light blue is one of his favorites, he has developed techniques for about eighty other colors, greatly increasing what can be achieved in

the medium. This expanded palette made possible such projects as the decoration of large surfaces including the walls of a restaurant, the inside of a hotel lobby, and the doors of an elevator.

More often than not, his work combines several different colors and patterns, both amorphous and geometrical. The façade of his *Four-Drawer Box* usually presents a different color for each drawer. Instead of one consistent color as on *The Boat Box*, another variation of the boat form featured vertical strips in six colors. Even his bowls feature multiple colors. He decorated the inside of a red bowl with a striking plant-like form suggesting a starfish. His small, square boxes are embellished with multicolored

Orange Boat, H. 13" W. 18" L. 45". Kubo created *Orange Boat* by applying urushi lacquer to the wood. The horns in Kubo's works are created with various woods, including cedar, pine and zelkova, painted with urushi lacquer, and then covered with gold and silver.

stripes, checks, or amorphous amoeba-like forms. The surface on another box recalls the pattern of a Piet Mondrian painting.

His fame has spread to America where he has exhibited dining tables, side tables, and small chests of drawers. Several years ago, he collaborated with a Philadelphia furniture maker, Michael Hurwitz, on a desk and other furniture. Hurwitz, known for his Japanese-inspired work, made the furniture, and Kubo applied the lacquer.

Conceived about five years ago, *The Boat* is part of a series. He got the idea for the shape from the movie *20,000 Leagues Under the Sea*, based on the Jules Verne novel about the submarine *Nautilus*. The gold-leafed teeth projecting from the lid recall similar

Kubo's fame has spread to America where he has exhibited dining tables, side tables, and small chests of drawers. Several years ago, he collaborated with a Philadelphia furniture maker, Michael Hurwitz, on a desk and other furniture.

shapes on the back of the *Nautilus* or maybe the spine of a dinosaur. Kubo wants them to suggest speed.

To make the boat's body, Kubo cut beech, the traditional wood for weapons, into thin strips and wound them around a mold. After sealing the beech with a coat of lacquer, he glued cloth to the surface using rice paste and lacquer. Then he applied a

Silver Boat, H. 22" W. 18" L. 34". Kubo created *Silver Boat* by applying charcoal power, silver powder, and urushi lacquer to thin wood. The horns in Kubo's works are created with various woods, including cedar, pine and zelkova, painted with urushi lacquer, and then covered with gold and silver.

ground of finely crushed clay, raw lacquer, and more rice paste using special spatulas to create a dappled effect. The process requires up to fifty applications of pigmented lacquer, clear lacquer, and other coatings to achieve the hard, smooth, vibrantly colored façade. Unlike normal paint, the lacquer needs a humid atmosphere and several days to dry between coats. Then the lacquer must be laboriously rubbed down to a smooth surface, which reveals the different colors and patterns.

The polishing and burnishing process is called *senbenkoguri*, which means, "to polish a thousand times." The Japanese often refer to Tsugaru lacquer as *Baka Nuri*, which translates as "Idiot's Lacquer." It is not a pejorative term but rather, recognition that perhaps only an idiot would spend so much time making a single piece. While Kubo's small box took about seven months to make, some work can take two years. Even Commodore Perry would have been impressed.

Four-Drawer Box, 2007. Paulownia, plywood, urushi lacquer; H. 8¼" W. 10" D 5". Kubo likes to make boxes in delicate sizes. Most have lids making *Four-Drawer Box* unique among his works.

PO SHUN LEONG

Born: 1941, Northhampton, England

Viewers Reference, Interpret, Experience

"Surprised," "astonished," and "amazed" describe typical reactions to Po Shun Leong's *Landscape Box*. But even those words do not convey its full emotional impact. Made with at least sixteen different types of wood sawn into hundreds of shapes and sizes, the box contains twenty-one compartments and one secret space. The

---

Leong's boxes, like his furniture and sculpture, are directly influenced by the early twentieth century constructivism of such artists as Kazimir Malevich, Wassily Kandinsky, Aleksandr Archipenko, and Naum Gabo.

---

bottom third of the façade pulls out to reveal a large drawer flanked by additional delights. Leong relishes the idea of the hidden treasure.

On the most mundane level, Leong insists *Landscape Box* is meant to be used and create its own history. But the piece also is about construction, destruction, and the rise and fall of civilizations. Leong has repeated the theme in his furniture and the fifty or so landscape boxes he has made since the first one in 1986. Titles such as *Rise and Fall of the City of Mahoganny*, *Pompeii Vessel*, *Mesa Verde*, and *Set of Two Coffee Tables* (held together by bolts recovered from the Berlin Wall), interpret and reinterpret that theme. Indeed, the box is encrusted with numerous shapes that recall ancient landmarks such as Petra in Jordan, Delphi in Greece, the Dim-Moon City of Delight in Baghdad, the Mont St. Michel cathedral in

ABOVE
Po Shun Leong in his studio with parts for his boxes.

OPPOSITE
Landscape Box, 2008. Buckeye, Philippine mahogany, pau amarillo, pink ivory wood, Honduran mahogany, ebony, palm wood, wengé, lacewood, pernambuco, holly, bocote, purple heart, maple, apple; H. 28½" W. 21" D. 13½".

France, the Potala fortress of the Dali Lama in Tibet, the Stupa pinnacles in Burma, the Inca city of Machu Picchu in Peru, and the temple of the Giant Jaguar at Tikal in Guatemala.

The natural woods at the cabinet's base suggest the primeval nature upon which the towers, steps, arches, and other fragments of man's monuments are piled. Once the chaotic mass of past civilizations rises to the crest, the composition becomes more rational and high tech, with four turbine forms (Leong calls them "antennae") that create a crown. Is this an optimistic statement about human progress and our modern technological society? That is the beauty of good art. Different individuals are inspired to bring their own interpretation to the subject, and here there is much to interpret.

ABOVE LEFT

Crescent Box, 1983. Hawaiian Koa; H. 9". W. 12". D. 7". One of Leong's first production boxes made soon after his arrival in the United States, *Crescent Box* had a simple design but was time consuming to make.

ABOVE RIGHT

Figure, 2002. Honduran mahogany; H. 60". A visit to an exhibition of the playful sculptures by the early twentieth century German artist, Max Ernst, inspired this piece. The faces in the head rotate to change the expression. She nurtures the golden egg in her belly.

Leong's resume is diverse. He was born in Northampton, England, to parents who emigrated from China before World War II. Like many children in wartime London, Leong was sent to live with friends in the country. Leong remembers spending hours playing with a detailed model of an ocean liner the friend had made, and the experience helps explain his fascination with the complex shapes that cover his boxes.

After graduating from a Quaker high school in England, he briefly studied sculpture at the Royal College of Art. Realizing he was more suited to architecture and design, he transferred and in 1964 earned a degree in architecture. One summer, he won a scholarship to study with the French modernist architect, Le Corbusier, and visited the classical icons of western architecture in Rome, Italy, and Greece; the great medieval cathedrals in

Europe; and the modernist buildings built after World War II.

He practiced architecture for a short time in London before volunteering with the American Friends Service Committee to serve in a mountain village several hours from Mexico City. He worked with villagers

---

The artistic aspects of the box are full of references and interpretations, but there is more to experience. All wood is carefully chosen with an artist's eye for color.

---

to dig a well, build a bridge, market their weaving, and help improve their lives. After a year, he took a job with the Mexican government. His challenge was to design school buildings that could be built with locally available materials, minimal tools, and carpenters with limited skills. He stayed in Mexico for sixteen years, designing twenty-seven prefabricated schools as well as numerous residential and commercial buildings. To relax, he painted local landscapes.

While in Mexico, Leong began designing chairs. Some of his chairs were produced commercially for Mexican resort hotels. One low-cost design using palm leaves woven on a wooden frame sold 10,000 sets. By 1981, a new Mexican president had been elected, and the economy deteriorated. Leong moved his family to California and pursued chair design. Buying a house in

Metropolis, 2006. Mainly mahogany, maple, ebony; H. 73" W. 31" D. 19". *Metropolis*, an assemblage of tall containers with many drawers and internal lighting, evokes the work of Naum Gabo.

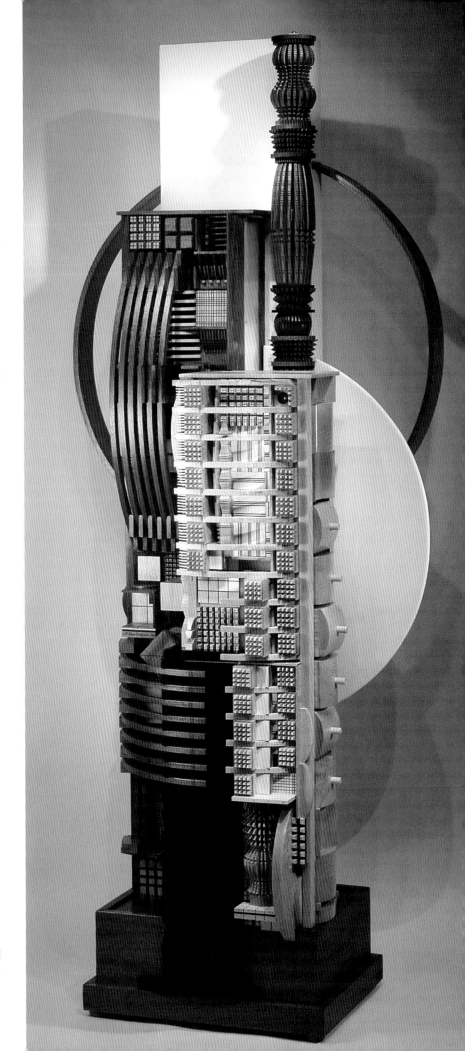

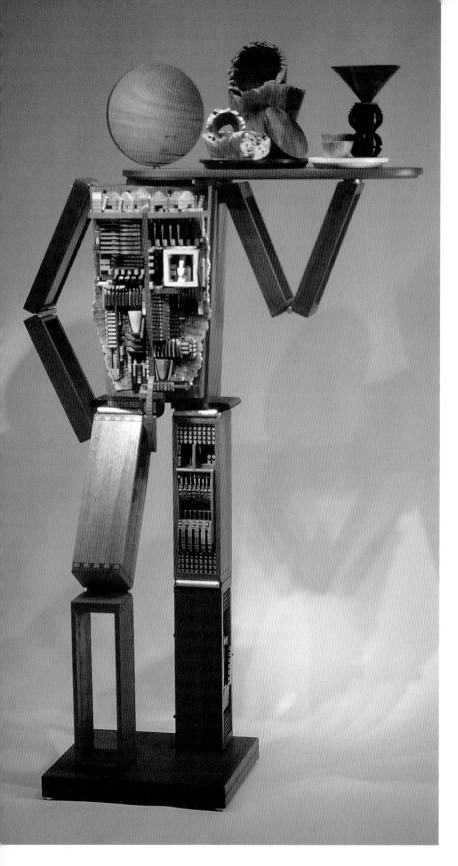

Waiter, 2002. Mainly mahogany; H. 72" W. 48" D. 15". The *Waiter*, who is the same height as woodturner Bob Stocksdale, is holding scrap turnings from his friend's workshop. A wine compartment is concealed in the figure's chest. The sculpture *Waiter* was made for the Furniture Society's 2003 *Cabinets of Curiosities* exhibition.

Winnetka near Los Angeles, he built a small studio where he worked on chair models. After leaving Mexico, he received the Daphne award for excellence in furniture design from the Hardwood Institute.

Leong's first boxes, such as *Crescent Box*, featured smooth, curved surfaces that required time-consuming sanding and finishing. He began to cut numerous shapes and forms, filling bins with an infinite variety of parts that he glued onto his increasingly complex boxes. As they got bigger and bigger, he started to make full-size desks, chairs, consoles, and coffee tables using the same techniques. Some of his most unusual work took the form of abstract people like *Figure*, which was inspired by the playful sculpture of the German Surrealist, Max Ernst; *Football*, which suggested a life-size soccer player with ball; and *Waiter*, which featured a figure carrying a tray of rough turnings given to him by Bob Stocksdale.

Leong's boxes, like his furniture and sculpture, are directly influenced by the early-twentieth-century constructivism of such artists as Kazimir Malevich, Wassily Kandinsky, Aleksandr Archipenko, and Naum Gabo. The influence is clear in Leong's art where he, like the Constructivists, builds his work piece by piece rather than the traditional method of carving the entire shape out of a solid block of wood or marble.

Leong's compositions are subtly compartmentalized. In *Landscape*, the natural base, the chaotic detritus of civilization, and the rationality of modern times are all framed by walls of nature represented

Desk, 1996. Cherry burl; H. 84" W. 48" D. 15". Leong became famous for his boxes and decided to scale them up into full-size furniture. Centered in the desk is a white city rising into a landscape of columns, pyramids, and hills. A golden orb, symbol of harmony and power, sits in the crest.

Landscape Box, 2008. Pink ivory, various other woods; H. 24" W. 20"
D. 10". *Landscape Box* is one of a series of more than fifty different
containers that Leong first began making in 1986. The rare pink ivory
wood sets off the front of the multi-drawer box.

Ancient City, 2006. Many woods; H. 15" W. 15" D. 10". *Ancient City*, with small drawers, was originally a boat-like structure that was drastically deconstructed. It was again modified for the 2006 Furniture Society Exhibition called *Show Me Your Drawers*.

by buckeye burl. The base and Philippine mahogany sides of the box are articulated with regular squares and columns. The steps that wind from bottom to top guide the eye around the ruins.

The artistic aspects of the box are full of references and interpretations, but there is more to experience. All wood is carefully chosen with an artist's eye for color. Some maple components are painted white to provide a focal point while others are gilded to catch light.

Leong also at times makes use of historical wood: a slice of apple wood certified to be from the last known living tree planted by Johnny Appleseed in Ohio; and a chunk cut from a branch of the Southern magnolia planted by President Andrew Jackson at the White House in early 1828 in honor of his deceased wife, Rachel.

Even Leong suggests *Landscape* might be viewed as "slightly gaudy or over the top," but he explains that even the Parthenon was originally painted in bright colors, as were parts of the Forbidden City in Beijing. He has added a Western point of view by inserting a section of white painted elements in the interior. Is that the popular view of Greek temples or is it shades of Elsie de Wolfe, the trendy, early-twentieth-century interior designer who painted everything white? Look again and discover more and more references to ponder.

PETER LLOYD

Born: 1952, London, England

'What If?' Brings Innovations

What if a piece of wood were crimped like a sheet of paper? Peter Lloyd is always asking the "what if" question that will lead him to a new design. In this case, he conceived a box whose lid suggested a puckered lip, a moue, or a pout. All of the curves in *Moue, Box No. 1147* were cut with an Arbortech wood-shaping tool, which works like a chainsaw. The box is joined together

All photos by Peter Lloyd.

Lloyd's designs have changed only gradually over time. He does not jump from one big idea to another but rather refines them slowly.

---

with blind tenons and dowels, their ends proud of the surface. The interior holds two levels of dovetailed walnut trays. The box itself is made of yew from a tree cut down by a friend for his then-girlfriend, who was building an addition to her house.

Another box called *Creased* featured a curve even more pronounced than the puckered lips—almost a breaking wave. Occasionally, Lloyd sets an agate in the lid as a handle, or a circular inlay in the surface. Such details, along with his signature wooden hinges, are about as ornamented as his boxes get.

Instead, he likes the wood, particularly British woods, to be the center of attention. In contrast to his friend Andrew Crawford (page 61), who makes his boxes to decorate, Lloyd's work celebrates wood. In fact, like American cabinetmaker James Krenov, Lloyd lets the rough board suggest the ultimate design. Dark English

ABOVE

Peter Lloyd in his workshop in Cumbria, England.

OPPOSITE AND BELOW

Moue, Box No. 1147, 2008. Yew, black walnut, velvet; H. 5" W. 13" D. 8".

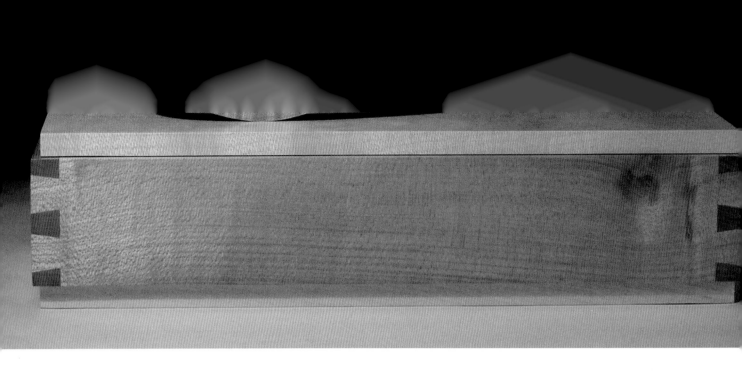

Crescent Box, 2008. Elm, Sycamore; H. 3" W. 10" D. 4". Maybe the adornment above *Crescent Box* is a smiley face, maybe a boat, or perhaps it is a crescent moon.

burl oak becomes a robust box, while lighter sycamore calls for a more restrained design. There are plenty of English species to choose from so he sees no need to use exotic woods from threatened rain forests. While the boxes themselves are straightforward, his

Lloyd took a circuitous journey on the way to becoming a full-time box maker.

prominent wooden hinges and the highly figured wood—often with a free edge—provide the interest.

Lloyd's designs have changed only gradually over time. He does not jump from one big idea to another but rather refines them slowly. His early boxes had silver-plated hinges. He hid the chains that held the lid open by cutting channels in the box sides. Wanting to make everything himself, Lloyd made his own wooden-strap hinges, small hinges on the back of the box, or hinges that pivoted on dowels.

At first, he hand-cut the dovetails, but in order to speed up production, he developed a router-table method using plastic spacers. Some boxes are mitered with decorative splines at the corners. One of his most expensive boxes has a complex hidden catch that opens when two magnets contained in the box are placed in just the right position. All of his boxes are sanded to a smooth, glassy finish and coated with Danish oil and wax to achieve an inviting tactile surface. Most boxes for men are lined with leather, while those for women are fitted with silk and velvet.

Lloyd has made twenty or thirty boxes with oak from *HMS Victory*, Admiral Horatio Nelson's famous flagship from the Battle of Trafalgar. An entrepreneur purchased a supply of the wood when the ship was being refurbished, and distributed it to English craftsmen so they could make limited editions to commemorate the 200th anniversary of the battle in 2005. Although it is difficult to work because of rot and worm holes, Lloyd bought enough extra to make another six boxes.

Lloyd also has made a box out of teak removed during restoration of *HMS Trincomalee*, the oldest British warship afloat (*HMS Victory* is older, but in dry dock). Built in 1817 in India, the frigate is now preserved at Hartlepool, on the east coast of Britain. The box was for a client whose ancestor had helped build the ship.

Since 1990, when Peter Lloyd Fine Hardwood Boxes was born, he has made more than 1,100 boxes for every occasion and use. In addition to the standard jewelry, laptop, cash, and work boxes for sewing, he also constructs special ones to hold family heirlooms, bibles, christening objects, chess

sets, and corporate gifts. His stationery boxes have drawers. *Box No. 27* (he numbers each one consecutively), made for a vicar, holds the chalice and plate used to give communion to housebound parishioners.

Until a couple of years ago, Lloyd avoided ring boxes because he could not come up with a design he really liked. Responding to repeated requests, he finally hit on a design with a curved back and top, and straight front and sides. The prototype required about the same amount of work as a larger box. To sell it at a reasonable price, he simplified the design, making it square (his wife had criticized the irregular shape of the prototype) and fitted it with a wooden hinge and a magnetic catch.

Jewelry Box, 2008. Burl oak, ripple sycamore; H. 4" W. 12" D. 7½". In *Jewelry Box*, Lloyd particularly likes the contrast between the precisely made dovetail joints on the sycamore trays and the raw-edged burl oak.

Lloyd took a circuitous journey on the way to becoming a full-time box maker. He recalls making a cheese board as a Christmas present for his grandmother at the age of ten. He vividly remembers how he sanded and sanded that board just like he sands his boxes today. His father was an architect and had a basement full of home-repair tools. He made his first box at age nineteen, for his first girlfriend.

After high school, Lloyd took a job as an air traffic controller assistant at Heathrow Airport. He enjoyed the view from the tower but grew bored and left for Scotland to work in a hotel because he hoped to learn to ski. He soon discovered Scotland lacks snow, so he went off to hotel and catering school. That field was too frenetic so he tried the retail clothing business, but could never figure out what an assistant merchandiser was supposed to do.

Lloyd kept remembering how much he had liked woodworking in school, so he decided to become a woodworking instructor. He got a job with a manufacturer of door jambs and went part-time to become certified as a craft design teacher. During that time, he made another box for the woman who would eventually become his wife. After he received his teaching certificate, the couple and their new baby moved to Cumbria, where he took a job teaching. After about four years, he figured out he did not do well with authority figures, and decided to do something more interesting. The family moved to Botswana, where he taught woodworking and his wife worked as a nurse.

Returning home to Cumbria after two years, Lloyd decided to go to work for himself. At first, he reproduced pine furniture and mirror frames in a garden

Antidote to Computers, 2007. Burl oak; H. 3½" W. 12" D. 7". Lloyd made *Antidote to Computers* for his son's graduation from the university with a degree in multimedia computing. It took a while to find a piece of wood with a natural opening for the circuit board.

Twins, 2007. Bog oak, ripple sycamore; H. 17" W. 15" D. 9". Lloyd calls *Twins* his skeleton box. The idea came from the inside out. He started with the trays, decided they could be drawers, and got to thinking about the bare minimum of material needed to support them.

aviary he converted into a shop. Trying to find something more interesting to make, he kept looking at a four-foot plank of burl oak. About this time, he attended a craft fair in nearby Carlisle and saw boxes for sale for a hundred pounds. What if he made a box with the oak? He did, and when a friend wanted to buy it, he got a feeling like a shot of adrenaline. Another friend ran a local craft fair and asked him to participate. That all these events came together at once he considers fate, and a sign that he was destined to make boxes.

Lloyd now sells most of his boxes over the Internet, and he no longer works in a drafty aviary. He has built a proper workshop attached to his house in Cumbria. But with his success, the workshop has become crowded, and he has had to use up even the last bit of ceiling space to store rolls of velvet. And his mind is crowded too—with ideas for boxes. Some of the ideas result from mistakes. Several years ago, he made five trays for a box, all the wrong size. He always fabricates the box first, and then the trays, so using them for a box was not an option. But what if Lloyd used them as drawers? They became *Twins*. What if?

TOM LOESER

Born: 1956, Boston, Massachusetts

Pioneer Pushes Boundaries

Tom Loeser's boxes rock, which is no surprise because there is a kinetic aspect to much of his work. His first furniture to win public recognition was a trio of chairs that folded flat to hang on the wall in the manner of nineteenth-century Shaker chairs suspended from pegs. He liked the design morphing from a two-dimensional

Since his days at Boston University, Loeser has researched traditional furniture so he can "turn the historical furniture inside out or upside down or backward."

wall hanging to a three-dimensional functional object. His *Roller* series turns the concept of opening a blanket chest on its head. Instead of the lid lifting up, the chest itself rolls out from under the stationary top. His museum seating rotates 360 degrees to afford a panoramic view of the gallery, while at the same time forcing visitors to interact with their neighbors while deciding how far to turn.

Movement and interactivity also permeate his drawer-filled cabinets. A few are straightforward, like *Four by Four*, a chest in the Smithsonian's Renwick collection that is a composition of eight drawers decorated in thirty-four alternating tones of blue, green, purple, and yellow. Others have multiple drawers in various sizes, some with drawers set sideways within another drawer. A few are more complex—one horizontal wall cabinet, for example, features five drawers that slide sideways

ABOVE

Tom Loeser works on *Eddy*, which is constructed from white oak, sitka spruce, and birch plywood.

OPPOSITE AND BELOW

Cyrano (bottom, and below right) and *Roxane* (top, and below left), 2008. Mahogany; H. 10" W. 29" D. 5½" (each box).

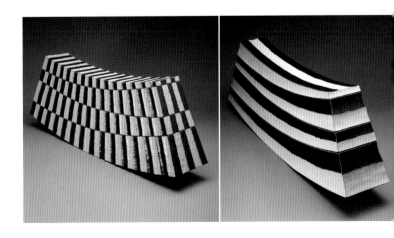

LEFT

*Multiple Complications,*1995. Wood and paint; H. 50" W. 34" D. 21". *Multiple Complications* seems like a generic chest, but the inside spaces get complicated with drawers inside of drawers inside of drawers. To find the extra drawer requires exploration.

BELOW

Multiple Complications (detail). You can find the side door only after a lot of looking.

to expose five more drawers. The idea is to force the viewer to play with the object and discover the surprises that wait inside.

Since his days in the Program in Artisanry (PIA) at Boston University, where he took an influential course from antique specialist John Kirk, Loeser has researched traditional furniture so he can "turn the historical furniture inside out or upside down or backward." His *LadderbackcabreddaL* chair does just that by joining two standard ladderbacks, a rocker resting on the ground and a side chair rising upside-down from the rocker's crest rail. The piece can be used as a rocker or flipped over to become a side chair.

Sometimes, the material is not traditional, as with his cardboard boxes. The cardboard produced a grain pattern like wood, only coarser, and he carefully cut dovetails to join the boxes as sort of a visual pun. For public seating at the Madison Museum of Contemporary Art he wrapped wide strips of industrial felt around the building's columns, and cinched the material in place with steel straps.

His latest work is not furniture but rather sculpture based on boat-building techniques. In 2005, the University of Wisconsin Wood/Furniture Program hosted Josh Swan, a traditional boat builder. The next year, following designs of Maine boat builder Platt Montfort, Loeser and two graduate students built their own skiffs with oak ribs and fir stringers covered with heat-shrunk Dacron skins. Out of this experience grew *Flotilla*, a series of sculptures made up of ribs and stringers, complete with seats but no skin, that take seven different configurations including a circle, an arch, a corkscrew, and a squiggle.

Loeser has even made furniture out of paper. In the late-1990s, he designed silk-screened and wood-block prints that could hang on the wall, or could be cut out and folded to create miniature chests. Lamps, wall clocks, and jewelry complete his repertoire, but there is no telling what he might come up with next.

Loeser has been making stacking boxes for years. The idea may have taken root after a six-month visit to Japan in 1993, where he saw traditional stacked lacquer boxes.

The Japanese manufacture them in plastic, as children's lunch boxes. He has always enjoyed making band-sawn boxes à la Art Carpenter, the first generation

---

Loeser pioneered the idea of painting wood art. Because the material is mostly brown, paint is necessary to use the whole color wheel.

---

studio furniture maker who pioneered the idea, but the challenge is making them so they do not look band-sawn.

For *Cyrano* and *Roxane*, he started with two chunks of mahogany, cut the sides off, and then cut angles on each of the sides. He then sliced the mahogany blocks horizontally to form the lids, then again to

Cardboard Box #1, 1990. Corrugated cardboard, colored paper; H. 15" W. 23" D. 14". Corrugated cardboard is a completely non-precious material. In *Cardboard Box #1,* Loeser achieved various surface effects by cutting the cardboard at different angles. The color comes from colored paper glued to the cardboard before it is cut.

form the individual compartments. After all of the parts were glued together, the surfaces were carved and painted. It all took much longer than he expected because of multiple angles and curves.

Although both boxes are the same size, the interior configurations differ, as do the paint and carving. The horizontal-striped box recalls the long nose of Cyrano de Bergerac, while the flashier vertical-striped box conjures the beautiful but unattainable Roxane from the nineteenth century play.

Inspired by Alphonse Mattia, his teacher at PIA, Loeser pioneered the idea of painting wood art. Because the material is

mostly brown, paint is necessary to use the whole color wheel. Studying the work of color theorist, Joseph Albers, Loeser became particularly interested in the way adjacent colors interact.

Loeser originally thought he would paint the boxes black and white, but at the last minute, he decided to experiment with color. Red, blue, and green milk paint delineate the three compartments in the horizontally striped box, while he added purple as a fourth color to the vertically striped one. The carving, done with an angle grinder fitted with chainsaw discs, enhances the painted pattern and guides the eye. Sanding between each coat abraded the edges of the cuts to expose the red mahogany that hints at a third color. He first started using the technique on his blanket chests.

Loeser's interest in color may be traced back to his high school ceramics teacher. After graduation, he worked for a year in a production ceramic shop before going off to Haverford College in Philadelphia. Following graduation, he visited his friend Mitch Ryerson, who was attending PIA, and decided to enroll in the program himself. He thought it would be nice to have design skills but never imagined he could make a living at it.

Then, his folding chairs—a school project—were shown at the Workbench Gallery in New York City. To his surprise, people other than his mother and father wanted to buy his work. So, after earning his bachelor's degree in fine arts, he became a full-time cabinetmaker, spending nine

Eddy, 2008. White oak, Sitka spruce, birch plywood; H. 32" W. 32" D. 17". Loeser likens *Eddy*, a member of his *Flotilla* series, to the futility of a dog chasing its tail.

years working in the legendary Emily Street cooperative in Boston.

During that time, he filled in for faculty on sabbatical at Rhode Island School of Design. He realized he would need a master's degree if he wanted to continue teaching, so he enrolled in the University of Massachusetts program that was the successor to the Program in Artisanry. He got a job teaching at the California College of Arts and Crafts in Oakland in 1989, and two years later, an appointment to the University of Wisconsin. Since 1991, he has headed the university's Wood/Furniture Program.

At first, he used the school wood shop, but now Loeser works from a 900-square-foot facility on the outskirts of Madison, in an old sheet metal factory converted to artist studios. It is a fifteen-minute walk, or a five-minute bike ride, from his house. He is experimenting with making little model chairs he saws out of a single piece of wood. He stacks them in different configurations, like a complicated coral reef, and is trying to figure out if they can be scaled up into full-size objects. Loeser is always pushing the boundaries, and trying to see the world in a different way.

ABOVE

Chest of Drawers, 1989. Mahogany, poplar, Baltic birch, mahogany plywood; H. 73" W. 29" D. 24". Part of the Museum of Fine Arts Boston New American Furniture show, *Chest of Drawers* was based on an eighteenth century chest-on-chest Loeser saw in the collection. He deconstructed it and added a painted and carved surface.

MICHAEL MODE

Born: 1946, Quakertown, Pennsylvania

Taking Techniques to New Levels

Nothing from his childhood suggested Michael Mode would grow up to be a renowned woodturner and box maker. In contrast to most craftsmen, who started making things at a young age, Mode was a straight-A student who in his senior year in high school discovered creative writing. He attended Haverford College in Philadelphia thinking he might become a writer.

Frank Klausz was a particular influence on Mode. A Hungarian refugee, Klausz impressed Mode with his traditional cabinetmaking skills.

In college, he began to write poetry and discovered the joy of creating. It was as if someone flicked a switch, and Mode developed an insatiable urge to create. But he did not like the constraints of an academic life, so he took a leave of absence in his junior year and never went back. His mother and father had died when he was young, and with no one to push him, he did whatever he wanted.

His creative interest shifted from words to music as he taught himself to play piano and write music. In the early 1970s, he visited Morocco, where he saw an old man turning spindles on an ancient bow lathe. Back in Pennsylvania by 1975, he decided to try turning for himself and constructed a foot-powered lathe from an old treadle sewing machine.

That same year, he completed his first major woodworking project by assembling a harpsichord kit.

All photos by Michael Mode.

ABOVE

Michael Mode working at his lathe in his shop in Bristol, Vermont.

OPPOSITE

Akbar's Alias, 2008. Wengé, holly, yellow-heart, ebony; H. 13" W. 10½" D. 10½". The title *Akbar's Alias* references the sixteenth century Moghul emperor who ruled when the dome shape was popular in Indian architecture.

Although it was just a matter of following directions, the project showed him the possibilities of wood. He started making boxes, candlesticks, wooden bottles, Christmas ornaments, and some laminated work. Realizing he needed a motorized lathe, he bought a used one from local cabinetmaker, Ken Dieterly.

Several months later, Mode returned to show Dieterly some of his work and, impressed, the cabinetmaker, offered Mode a job making the bodies and necks for electric guitars. Laminating the curly maple, mahogany, and rosewood required precise work, and it provided good training. Mode fabricated guitar parts two days a week,

while making boxes and other items for himself on the side.

Around 1980, he met some local furniture makers who had decided to form a support group called Guild 10. One of its members, Frank Klausz, was a particular influence on Mode. A Hungarian refugee, Klausz impressed Mode with his traditional cabinetmaking skills and reinforced his obsession with precision workmanship. Also at this time, David Ellsworth, one of the foremost woodturners in the world, moved nearby. Mode learned from his example how one could make a living as a woodturning artist.

Akbar's Avenue, 2007. Holly, purpleheart, pink ivory wood, ebony, boxwood; H. 12" Dia. 6". Under the lid of *Akbar's Avenue* is a miniature checkerboard and chess set, complete with a pair of tweezers to move the tiny pieces.

In 1982, Mode was accepted into the American Craft Council show in Baltimore. After that, he continued doing four or five shows a year and selling wholesale to galleries all over the country. During this period, Mode was making boxes mostly out

---

Turned lamination goes back at least to the nineteenth century. Turners, including Lincoln Seitzman, who wanted to imitate the design of Indian baskets, revived it in the 1980s.

---

of burls and spalted wood, along with vase-like vessels with lids and a few with natural edges. He also turned Christmas ornaments by the thousands and created miniature chess sets. The carved pieces fit into their own box, which in turn fit under a larger dome that contained the board.

In 1992, Mode turned his first winged vessels with curved tips like a manta ray that have become a signature design. Soon he added lids to the vessels that recalled the domes in Indian Moghul architecture such as the Taj Mahal. Although he had lived in Kashmir, it was not until he saw the dome shapes in a book that he realized the connection. One's design vocabulary is often stored in the subconscious.

Because he was tiring of figured wood, Mode began to add abstract pattern to both the body and the dome by turning laminated blocks glued up of colorful tropical woods. These designs also came to him subconsciously, but were obviously derived from Islamic architecture in Kashmir.

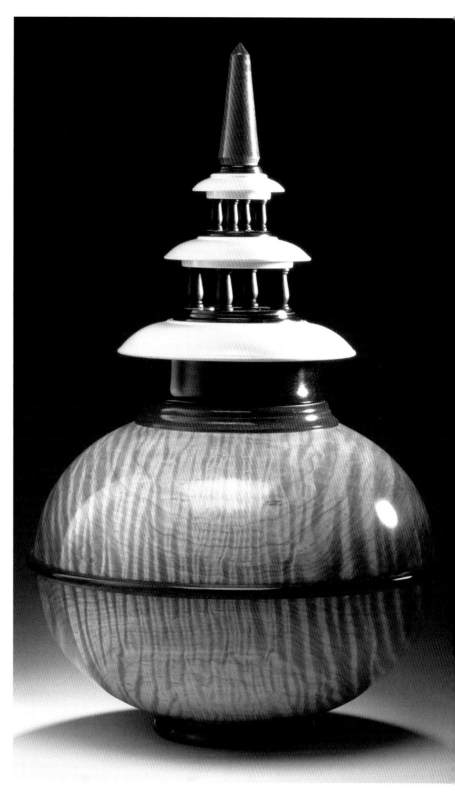

Hollywood Pagoda, 1996. Rosewood, curly maple, jarrah, holly, ebony, pink ivory wood; H. 19" Dia. 12". *Hollywood Pagoda* is another equator vessel turned in two parts and joined together to suggest an oriental pagoda.

Turned lamination goes back at least to the nineteenth century. Turners, including Lincoln Seitzman, who wanted to imitate the design of Indian baskets, revived it in the 1980s. The dramatic, abstract patterns in Mode's work, however, take the technique to a new level. *Intersections*, named for the pattern resulting from intersecting circles, was one of the last lidded, laminated vessels he turned.

In early 1999, Mode began to think about making lids using an old technique for turning bowls. The method involved turning a layered and glued blank comprised of concentric rings cut on an angle. After he learned the technique, he was so impressed by its possibilities that he abandoned the lids and focused instead on bowls. Although he cherishes the immediacy of the lathe, he is reconciled to spending up to half his time gluing up the blanks.

In addition to conserving precious tropical woods, the method lent itself to an endless variety of patterns. *Zebra Rising* and *Tut Tut*, for example, rely on black and white woods for effect, while the intersecting curves of *Rescued* conjure up a maze. Four different woods in *Take Off* clearly evoke a missile launch. *Optical Allusion* in holly has an almost transparent quality, while the grain of ziricote in *Behind the Scenes* suggests rows of receding hills.

When he is working on one project, he is always thinking about variations for the next one. Two years ago, he began playing with a technique of cutting his turned bowl in half and then gluing the two halves together on their upper edges to form a peaked shape like the Sydney Opera House. By starting with six bowls in graduated sizes, he can create twelve freestanding elements that can

be arranged in various sculptural groupings like *Walking Cathedrals*, made in 2008.

Focused on his ring-cut bowls, he made few winged vessels, but in 2005 lathe artist, Bin Pho, commissioned one, and he has continued to make them ever since. After he glues up the block that will produce the pattern, Mode turns the top to establish the shape and then flips over the wood to cut the bottom. A strobe light allows him to see the shape of the wing tips, which otherwise would appear as a blur like a rotating fan blade.

Once the parts have been assembled, he polishes away all the tool marks with the help of the lathe. After sealing the surface with superglue, he applies a French polish.

Mode believes everyone is born with ideas inside them that want to come out. He takes great pleasure in expressing his ideas in work of the highest precision. With his wife, fiber artist Lynn Yarrington, he shares a building adjacent to their home in Bristol, Vermont, overlooking the Adirondack Mountains. The chaos of his studio, the messy desk, and the crowded shop belay his highly organized and refined designs. Like Frank Sinatra, Mode is proud to say, "I did it my way."

Akbar's Affinity, 1998. Holly, ebony, pink ivory wood, purpleheart, wengé; H. 12" W. 19" D. 12". *Akbar's Affinity* is one of Mode's favorites in his *Winged Vessel* series. The piece reflects his interest in Moghul architecture.

CRAIG NUTT

Born: 1950, Belmond, Iowa

Seeing the Mundane in Different Light

Even as a child, Craig Nutt made things. His father and grandfather were tinkerers, and Nutt spent a lot of time in their workshops. After graduating from the University of Alabama in 1972 with a liberal arts degree, Nutt began restoring antiques. He learned cabinetmaking by studying old furniture, reading books on antiques and workshop texts, and gleaning tips from experienced cabinetmakers. British woodworkers such as Charles Hayward, Peter Child, and Frank Pain, and the British magazine *Woodworker* provided technical insights and an

Nutt embodies more direct social commentary in works such as Reliquary, *a miniature satin-lined, domed coffin that contains a cast bronze globe representing the world.*

array of unfamiliar terms like cramps, stopping, and glasspaper. Reading articles in the newly established *Fine Woodworking* magazine and attending craft conferences introduced him to American colleagues. By 1977, he became a full-time cabinetmaker selling traditional rocking chairs and other furniture. At the seminal 1979 and 1980 wood conferences at Purchase College near New York City, he met studio furniture makers Wendy Maruyama and Bob Trotman and attended seminars by luminaries such as Tage Frid, Wendell Castle, Sam Maloof, and wood turner Rude Osolnik.

Nutt got the idea for his signature "flying vegetables," "vege tables," and chairs from his college days when he

ABOVE

Craig Nutt in his studio with a model of one of his pieces on the bench.

OPPOSITE

Chocolate-Covered Donut Teapot, 2000. Mahogany; H. 13" W. 16" D. 3¾".

organized a marching band whose members dressed up as vegetables and played homemade instruments. Also an avid gardener, he sees his vegetable imagery as an accessible and metaphorical vocabulary that imparts humor, parody, and satire. Upon hearing Vice President George H. W. Bush in the 1988 presidential campaign state he would not use food as a weapon, Nutt began making hanging sculptures shaped like ears of corn to suggest vegetable bombers. After seeing whirligigs in a local museum, he expanded his repertoire to include whirligigs of carrots, corn, cayenne peppers, and other vegetables. It was a short step to vegetable furniture.

Nuclear Medicine Chest, 1984. Wood, detuned music box movement; H. 12" W. 5" D. 4½". Inspired by a cartouche box from King Tutankhamen's tomb, *Nuclear Medicine Chest* plays "Raindrops Keep Fallin' on My Head," with one note out of tune, as missiles cross the horizon. It has two drawers for aspirin and iodine capsules.

Photo by Craig Nutt.

Nutt embodies more direct social commentary in works such as *Reliquary*, a miniature satin-lined, domed coffin that contains a cast bronze globe representing the world. His bomb-shaped *Nuclear Medicine Chest* is fitted with a music box that plays an off-key "Rain Drops Keep Falling on My Head" while missiles go over the horizon.

After Nutt's wife took a job in Nashville, Tennessee, in 1998, the couple moved from downtown Northport, a bedroom community for Tuscaloosa, to a nine-acre farm in Kingston Springs. He resides only a few hundred feet from his gardens and his 3,000-square-foot studio and gallery, which he and a few close friends built. In contrast to his good friend Michelle Holzapfel, a turner who resides in Vermont and has access to beautiful burl woods, Nutt buys pine and poplar from the local lumber yard, or salvages blown-down trees and then has to figure out how to make the nondescript wood into something.

Nutt thinks of his boxes, and sometimes his cabinets, as objects that contain important ideas. Though his *Pepper* cabinet, at seven feet high, is not really a box, it offers the same sense of surprise when it is opened. Because the cabinet was commissioned as a donation to a museum in memory of a friend, Nutt built in a secret compartment to contain a research paper that the two had written. Craig compares his approach to H. C. Westerman, whose boxes also contain unexpected surprises.

Nutt designed his first sculptural boxes in the early 1980s. Along with some straightforward ones containing items such as presentation gavels, he produced a series

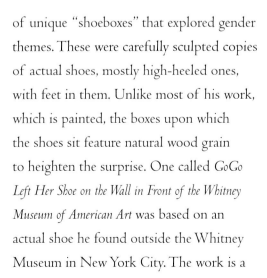

of unique "shoeboxes" that explored gender themes. These were carefully sculpted copies of actual shoes, mostly high-heeled ones, with feet in them. Unlike most of his work, which is painted, the boxes upon which the shoes sit feature natural wood grain to heighten the surprise. One called *GoGo Left Her Shoe on the Wall in Front of the Whitney Museum of American Art* was based on an actual shoe he found outside the Whitney Museum in New York City. The work is a

reference to Samuel Beckett's play, *Waiting for Godot*, where Vladimir leaves his shoes on the road for another traveler only to rediscover them himself.

The concept for *Donette Teapot* grew out of a carving exercise he assigned while teaching. The brief was to make something that began with a particular letter of the alphabet. That day the letter was D. Before class, he had picked up a bag of donuts so he decided to carve three powdered sugar coated donuts that became a teapot. Donuts are an iconic southern food with Krispy Kreme shops all over the region. So, the idea was fresh in his head when he was asked to make another teapot for a show. It was not such a goofy idea because he was following in the time-honored tradition of novelty ceramic teapots.

Wanting to make his wooden teapot functional, Craig equipped it with two

ABOVE LEFT

Carrot Cabinet, 2000. Turned, carved, and painted wood; H. 42" W. 9" D. 9". The door on the front of *Carrot Cabinet* opens to access three shelves.

ABOVE RIGHT

Radish Table, 2004. Oil paint on turned and carved wood; H. 29" W. 24" D. 24". *Radish Table* behaves more like a box. Rather than dropping down, the table leaves drop up to allow access to the interior of the radish.

Corncorde, 1996. Carved and painted wood; H. 36" W. 120" D. 120". *Corncorde* was commissioned to hang in the Atlanta International Airport as part of a large public arts project for the Atlanta Olympics. It is ten feet long with a "shuckspan" of ten feet.

compartments like a traditional tea caddy. He sized the compartments to hold teabags to reinforce the concept of fast food and fast tea. His chocolate and powdered sugar-covered donuts, icons of pop culture, are juxtaposed with porcelain teapots, traditionally used in high society tea ceremonies.

Juxtaposing two disparate ideas is a theme that runs through all of his work. Although vegetables occasionally decorated furniture in the eighteenth century, Nutt uses them not primarily as decoration but as the actual structure of his furniture. In his series of tables with cement tops, he juxtaposes boring and often oppressive concrete with mahogany, the traditional wood for high-style furniture. In his *Helical Dance* sculpture for Shearing Plough Corporation, he depicts the molecular structure of interferon but places it on a garden arbor. His point is to force people to see mundane things in a different light. Before cooks throw a carrot into the pot, maybe they will stop a minute to look at it with fresh eyes.

The hole in the center donut was turned on a lathe, reaffirming his skills on that machine. He sawed out the two compartments and then glued the sides back on. Nutt carved the chocolate covering in relief and used a reciprocating hand tool fitted with a blunt nail, like

---

The concept for the Donette Teapot *grew out of a carving exercise to make something that began with a particular letter of the alphabet.*

---

a tiny jackhammer, to give the surface a cakey appearance. Other air-powered grinding tools textured the inside of the donut.

After applying a coat of flat alkyd enamel, Nutt scumbled different shades of artist colors over the surface to achieve a realistic rendering of donuts similar to the finishes on his vegetable carvings. Although he usually works with poplar, he selected mahogany for his teapot, thinking that its brown color might suggest browned cake. Thin mahogany strips hold the top in the proper position.

Although Nutt is still making vegetable furniture, he has not produced any "shoeboxes" for a few years. However, when he made the first teapot, he cut three mahogany blanks. Prominent teapot collectors purchased *Donette*, the first teapot, featuring three powdered sugar coated donuts. *Chocolate-Covered Donut Teapot* is still in his collection, while the blank for a third one sits in his shop awaiting the right inspiration.

BELOW TOP

Walnut High-Top, 1985. Walnut, maple, padauk. *Walnut High-Top* is fitted with a drawer in the toe and a compartment under the sweat sock.

BELOW BOTTOM

Donette Teapot, 1999. Mahogany; H. 9" W. 16" D. 4". *Donette Teapot* is actually a tea caddy designed to hold a selection of tea bags.

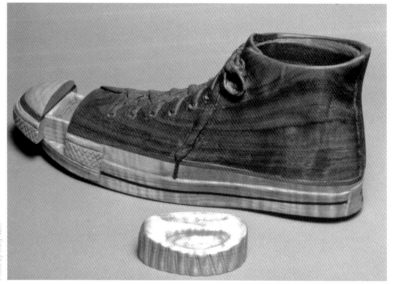

Photo by Craig Nutt.

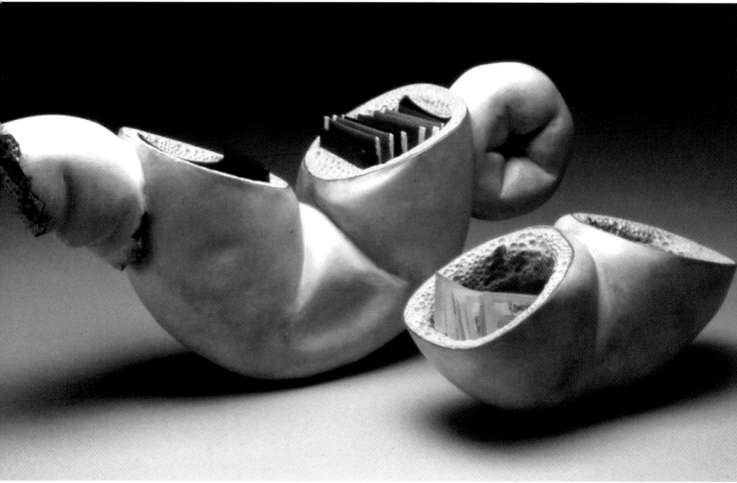

Photo by Bobby Hansson.

Jay and Janet O'Rourke

(Jay) Born: 1947, Santa Barbara, California
(Janet) Born: 1958, Los Angeles, California

Sharing a Beautiful Collaboration

Standing a foot and a half tall, *Vessel in Bloom* is among the most monumental boxes Janet and Jay O'Rourke make. Janet usually comes up with the idea, and then Jay has to figure out how to construct it—not always an easy task when the designs are so complex. Janet draws on her interest in ancient architecture, Asian art, Art Deco, and nature for her inspiration. The woods are selected for the beauty of their grain and for their contrasting colors.

The flower suggests a stylized wild rose complete with tiny black pearls attached to a turned disk with silver wire and applied to its center. Janet grew up surrounded by roses; they are her favorite flower. Jay and Janet like the motif so much they plan to carve more roses as separate pieces of jewelry to wear or display.

Jay turned the bowl and lid down to a thin wall while Janet carved the ebony. The light-colored beech, spalted

---

Jay sold turned miniature boxes along with the flatware and then began to make larger, square boxes. They were a runaway success.

---

because of a fungus in the tree, serves as a striking counterpoint to the dark ebony. After the parts were assembled with cyanoacrylate glue, the piece was sanded, finished with Danish oil, waxed, and given a high polish.

Growing up in Santa Barbara, Jay always made things with his hands—kid's forts, model cars, and toys. He often watched his father, who worked for the phone

Photo by Caitlin O'Rourke.

ABOVE

Jay and Janet O'Rourke.

OPPOSITE

Vessel in Bloom, 2008. Spalted Scottish beech, ebony, black pearls, sterling silver; H. 18" Dia. 8".

ABOVE LEFT

Pandora's Other Box,
2001. Purpleheart,
ebony, pink ivory,
pearls, gold leaf; H. 12"
W. 8" D. 6". Pandora's
box contained bad
things, but her other
box might have
contained good things
to spread peace, love
and happiness in the
world. The Pandora in
Pandora's Other Box is
a mermaid holding
pearls and wearing
1940s attire.

ABOVE RIGHT

Rabbit Rose, 2008.
Cocobolo, ebony,
betelnut, palm; H. 18"
Dia. 12". Janet always
loved rabbits. Rabbits
bring good luck, and
Rabbit Rose brings
good luck to the owner.

company, repair motorcycles. Jay took wood shop classes in school and, an avid surfer, ran his own surfboard repair business. As a teenager, he aspired to become a rock star, so it is not surprising that after about a year in a junior college art program, he became bored and dropped out.

After that experience, Jay began making things like Christmas cards, jewelry, and anything else he could sell at local craft shows. Although he initially liked jewelry the best, he switched over to wood in 1969 when show promoters told him they had too many jewelers and not enough woodworkers. He and a friend carved wooden flatware and chopsticks, initially in the living room of their apartment.

By 1972, they bought a lathe and taught themselves to turn bowls and plates to go with the flatware. The friend moved away to become a contractor, but Jay continued in the craft business.

Early on, Jay sold turned miniature boxes along with the flatware and then began to make larger square boxes. When they immediately became a runaway success, he took a break from turning and concentrated on constructed boxes. The glued-up containers have domed tops and sides cut on a band saw, and hinged lids pivoting on dowels, but customers could not resist the dazzling exotic woods. He makes them in all sizes from tiny ring boxes to women's jewelry cases lined with ultrasuede. Business card boxes are imprinted with the customer's logo. A few have gull-wing lids that pivot from the center of the box. All of the boxes, along with a line of folding letter openers also made from exotic woods, are available to the wholesale trade.

Janet met Jay—where else—at a Renaissance Craft Fair in San Francisco. Business was good, and Jay wanted to add carving to his boxes. He needed some extra help, so Janet worked in the Santa Barbara studio Jay shared with fellow box makers

---

Like their smaller hinged boxes, all of their turned vessels feature highly figured woods in contrasting colors.

Jeff and Katrina Seaton. Inspired by her mother, who is still painting at age eighty-three, Janet earned a bachelor's degree in illustration and completed some graduate work at Otis-Parson school of design in Los Angeles. She took to working with wood immediately, looking at carving as a way to draw in three dimensions. Jay and Janet were married in 1984.

After making hundreds of constructed boxes, Jay decided to set up the lathe again and began turning feet, drawer pulls, and other parts for some of their more complex drawer boxes. These included *Jaguar Offering*, a pyramid shape with five drawers, and *Pandora's Other Box*, a trapezoidal design with a single drawer. The pyramidal box was surmounted by a carved jaguar jumping over the moon, and the trapezoidal one featured Pandora standing on a turned hemisphere holding white pearls.

The hinged boxes and the folding letter openers continued to provide the bulk of the couple's sales, but gradually, turned vessels with carved finials supplanted the larger drawer boxes. Although they will still make them on commission, Jay and Janet for the past ten years have concentrated on turned vessels, which seem to complement Janet's carving better. Like their smaller hinged boxes, all of their turned vessels feature highly figured woods in contrasting colors, but they are also decorated with

Photo by Bob Barret

Bird in Flight, 2008 Spalted Scottish beech, ebony, piassaba palm, Taqua. Jay and Janet grew up on the California coast and remembrances of the birds flying across the sky as the sun set into the Pacific Ocean provided the inspiration for *Bird in Flight*.

Hinged Boxes, 1971–
2008. Smallest: H. ¾"
W. 1⅝" D. 1⅜" Largest:
H. 1¾" W. 5" D. 4¼". The
pieces displayed in
Hinged Boxes were all
Jay's original design.
The couple was among
the first to sell small,
exotic hardwood
boxes. The ebony end
caps serve as a frame
to highlight the highly
figured woods.

surface carving and finials such as birds, fish, and rabbits as well as leaves and feathers. *Man in the Moon* is topped with a face carved in a light-colored disk, and *Harlequin Heart* features a marquetry heart suggesting a jester's costume. *Raven Spirit* references a myth from Jay's Native American heritage; he is as a member of the Chumash Nation from the Santa Barbara area. Chumash cave paintings such as stylized arrows, suns, and zigzag motifs inspire carving on other vessels.

Not wanting to waste any precious exotic woods, the couple came up with a series of wall vases that also allowed Janet to show off her illustration skills. An ebony panel is attached to a pair of boards such as wengé, purpleheart, or cocobolo left over from the boxes. A space between the boards accommodates a hand-blown glass vial. Janet carves the ebony with her favorite animal and flower imagery and highlights the carving with gold leaf. While all of the designs show a subtle Asian influence,

this is overt in *Love and Enlightenment* where Chinese characters identifying the titles are included in the composition. Unfortunately, the scarcity of ebony and the lack of time have curtailed the production of these unique vases.

By the late 1990s, Santa Barbara had become expensive, so the O'Rourkes relocated to Hood River, Oregon. After raising a son and a daughter in Oregon, they recently moved again, this time to Paducah, Kentucky. They wanted to settle closer to their craft show venues on the East Coast and were persuaded to consider Paducah by Julie Shaw, a jeweler friend who runs a gallery there. When they saw the thriving art community, they bought a 150-year-old Victorian house in the Lower Town Arts District. They now work from a new studio in their backyard; Janet upstairs and Jay in his workshop on the first floor.

The couple has also opened Aspire Arts in the main house, where they live above the gallery. They show artists working in a number of different media including jewelry, glass, clay, and wood along with fine art. The gallery provides a venue for Janet to showcase her own colored pencil and mixed-media illustrations, which feature whimsical fairies and elaborate patterns and textures. Her work is shaped by fairy tales, Victorian design, and the work of Maxfield Parrish, the popular turn-of-the-twentieth-century illustrator. As art and costume director for a dance company in Hood River, she became fascinated with fairies in the production of *The Nutcracker* and *Swan Lake*. These fanciful creatures are scattered throughout her art and are featured in her recently published children's coloring book called *Fairy Dream*.

Jay and Janet compare the working of the wood to the cutting of fine gemstones. Jay turns the rough blocks of beautifully figured wood that become the elegant settings to display the gems that are Janet's carvings. This beautiful collaboration has flourished for more than a quarter of a century.

Dragonfly (detail), 1999. Pink ivory, Macassar ebony. This is the top of *Dragonfly*, a two-drawer, oval-shaped box with turned legs and turned pulls (inset). The couple believes that dragonflies are magical and wanted the box to be a special place to keep special things. *(From the Collection of Randy and Jennifer Price.)*

EMI OZAWA

Born: 1962, Tokyo, Japan

Mystery Evokes Viewer's Curiosity

Growing up in Tokyo, Emi Ozawa always enjoyed art. Her accountant father and her full-time homemaker mother encouraged her and sent her to art classes to nourish her interest. Inspired by her mother who loves to sew, Ozawa learned early to love creating things. While her two brothers played with trains, Ozawa built buildings out of blocks and walled cities with books.

Ozawa started out making both painted and unpainted furniture, often with animal themes.

Starting in kindergarten and all through school, she took art classes on Saturday mornings, learning watercolor, pen-and-ink drawing, paper collage, and oil painting.

An art education was almost preordained. Ozawa attended Joshibi University in Tokyo and then worked briefly as a graphic designer in an advertising agency. She enrolled in the Tokyo School of Arts in 1985, and initially aspired to become a sculptor. After two years, she transferred to the University of the Arts in Philadelphia as part of an exchange program. Ozawa wanted to make wooden sculpture that was strong enough for people to touch, but her early wood pieces were too fragile. Michael Hurwitz, who taught in the wood department in Philadelphia, convinced her that furniture could be both interactive and sculptural. As a result, she shifted her focus from sculpture to furniture. After receiving her bachelor's degree in fine arts in 1989,

ABOVE
Emi Ozawa in her studio painting ball lids her favorite color red.

OPPOSITE
Red Bridge, 2008. Maple plywood; H.20" W. 20" D. 3¼".

Ozawa earned a master's degree in fine arts from Rhode Island School of Design (RISD) in 1992.

After graduation, Ozawa worked part-time as a shop assistant for her former RISD teachers, Rosanne Somerson and Alphonse Mattia, at their shop in Dartmouth, Massachusetts. From Somerson, she learned the importance of fine craftsmanship, and from Mattia, she absorbed a sense of whimsy. At the same time, she started to show her own work at craft shows, and struck out on her own two years later. Although she now works independently in the woodworking

---

Ozawa delights in the fact that her work possesses a sense of mystery and evokes the viewers' curiosity.

---

cooperative that recently moved from New Bedford to Fall River, she enjoys the interaction with the eleven other craftsmen who share the space. The new shop is larger and closer to her home in Providence.

Ozawa started out making both painted and unpainted furniture, often with animal themes, such as her tall giraffe cabinet and her bird tables that sit on claws and whose tops fold up like wings. She gradually shifted to smaller painted items like circular mirrors, wall clocks, and particularly boxes. Her fascination with animals continues in some of these pieces such as her cat clocks, which, she explains, tell time by a whisker. Because these smaller pieces are faster to make and sell than large pieces of furniture, she can reach a wide audience. Though she still makes some pieces on commission, she

Cubic Circus, 1996. Mahogany, brass; H. 29" W. 15" D. 10". Ozawa started to name this piece *Antelope*, but she changed the name to *Cubic Circus* after the piece was finished when she saw the balancing act between the lid and the cubes.

Photo by Dean Powell.

LEFT

bOX, 2001. Poplar, maple; H. 4½" W. 2¾" D. 2¾". Ozawa once put a pebble on a stand as a gift for a friend. It was a short step to make the design into a box by drilling a hole in the cube and using a turned ball as a lid. This was the start of her box making.

has been concentrating on production items the last few years and creates about 500 objects annually.

Her boxes are more like playful children's toys than truly functional containers—they are toys for grown-ups, she says. They usually exhibit kinetic qualities reminiscent of mobiles by Alexander Calder, whose work she admires. Her early boxes were large in scale and more like furniture. *Rolling Saucers*, for example, rested on square legs, and its top was pulled open by a string attached to a brass rod with a saucer on each end that rolled down an incline built over the box top. *Pendulum Box* had a semicircular lid suspended from a brass rod that allowed the lid to oscillate back and forth. On *Quack-Quack*, the wide curved bill that serves as the lid is attached to a disk. When the disk is rotated, the top rises.

Ozawa delights in the fact that her work possesses a sense of mystery and evokes the viewers' curiosity, especially in the way the lids operate. She is more concerned about how they open than about what they contain. One of her most popular boxes,

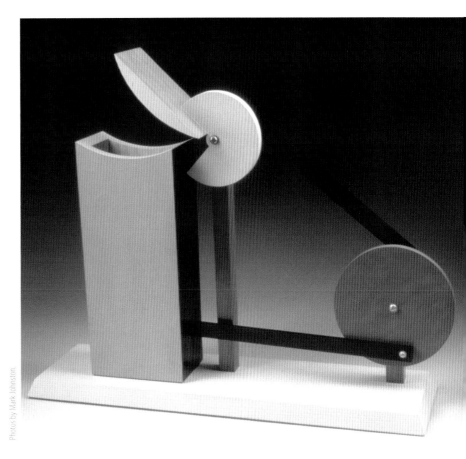

ABOVE

Quack-Quack, 1999. Maple plywood, cherry; H. 13" W. 17" D. 15". For *Quack-Quack*, Ozawa remembered an illustration of how Curious George transformed a broom and a ladder into a giraffe, and chairs into leopards and zebras. What began as a pencil box became a duck. The mechanism moves like a locomotive wheel.

Photos by Mark Johnston.

ABOVE TOP

Ring Box, 2005. Maple plywood; H. 6¾" W. 6¾" D. 2". *Ring Box* is a continuous hollow tube. When the lid in the upper section of the ring is removed, two openings appear, with the lid acting as a circuit breaker. The shape refers to both a finger ring and a circus ring.

ABOVE BOTTOM

Four Quarters, 2001. Cherry, magnet; H. 9" W. 9" D. 3". Awed by a shining full moon in the midnight sky, Ozawa made a series of moon-shaped boxes in mahogany. *Four Quarters* is a painted version.

a study in geometry, has a ball-shaped lid balanced on a cube-shaped box painted with multicolored triangles. The mystery is how the ball can stay perched there. Is it glued? Is there a magnet? Actually, it is an optical illusion because the ball rests on a slightly flattened surface.

Wound Up has another innovative lid. It is made up of five concentric circles in diminishing sizes that are pinned together so they swivel over the top to form a neat stack. The box itself also consists of hollowed circles in alternating colors, with the inside diameter gradually getting larger as the circles stack to form a cylinder.

Like most of her work, *Red Bridge* is part of a series of six. She started with her favorite shape, the circle. Whether a full moon or a Ferris wheel, circles remind her of completion, mobility, and balance. The circle of a microscopic egg that is the beginning of life is, for her, the original form.

Circles pervade her work. For example, *Four Quarters*, painted in four colors, is a circular box that rests on its edge like a wheel and comes apart in four sections. *Half Moon*, made in natural mahogany, takes the shape of half a circle while another box is shaped like a donut. *Seesaw 2* presaged *Red Bridge* with its open, semicircular base that supports a tiny box on each end. The upper section of *Red Bridge* recalls the lattice-like structure of cabinetry by Hurwitz. He in turn was strongly influenced by similar structures found in Japanese architecture.

To avoid the natural movement of wood, Ozawa cut the shape of the box out of stable maple plywood. She left the edges exposed because she likes the texture of the plies. Ozawa coats most of her work in bright colors, and red is one of her favorites. The top half of *Red Bridge* lifts off to expose an open compartment below, where tiny treasures can be stored.

When the piece was finished, she named it after a bridge because the upper half reminded her of trusses and the solid bottom section suggested a reflection in a river. Vaguely similar old red bridges are found in some Shinto shrines and traditional Japanese gardens. Perhaps unconsciously, they influenced her design, though she did not think about the connection until after she had finished the piece. Even the sturdiest bridges sway, and Ozawa enjoys the thought that few will resist the temptation to set *Red Bridge* rocking.

Seesaw 2, 2001. Maple plywood; H. 9" W. 19½" D. 8". Both a seesaw and a scale inspired *Seesaw 2*. Removing the lid sets the seesaw in motion.

ANDREW POTOCNIK

Born: 1963, Melbourne, Australia

Humbled by Nature's Beauty

Although Andrew Potocnik was born and reared in a suburb of Melbourne, Australia, he draws on the world, especially the Third World, for inspiration. His parents emigrated from Yugoslavia to Australia in 1950 after his father escaped from a concentration camp. Potocnik developed a love of wood from an early age and in high

Potocnik's multicultural Australian background helps him to understand other cultures, and his travels enable him to better appreciate his own environment.

school signed up for all the wood shop courses available. Despite his interest in woodworking, he did not want to enroll in a trade school. He opted for an art course, which led to a teaching degree, something he did not plan for, but a career he has enjoyed in combination with his drive to make art from wood.

Although he is now a full-time wood shop teacher, he has his own studio in the garage behind the house that his parents built. A creature of habit, Potocnik works in his shop for an hour or two every evening after school. The workspace, which he sometimes shares with nesting doves or possums, is filled with projects in various stages of completion. In between projects, he writes prolifically on woodturning topics such as product evaluations, exhibition reviews, and instructionals, many published in the *Australian Wood Review.*

ABOVE

Andrew Potocnik in his studio in Melbourne, Australia.

OPPOSITE

Multi-Axis Box V and *Multi Axis Box VI*, 2008. *V*: Red gum, gidgee, guitar string; H. 9" Dia. 2⅜". *VI*: Canthium, western myall, guitar string; H. 8" Dia. 2⅛".

Interactives, 2004.
Douglas fir;
H. 2" W. 9" D. 2".
After constructing
these forms with
their sandblasted
and limed surface,
Potocnik decided
to let individuals
arrange them
in whatever
configuration
they liked.

After the school year ends, Potocnik has the summer free to travel, study different cultures, and collect exotic woods. These trips have taken him to twenty-seven different countries in Asia and Africa, including thirteen trips to Nepal. He visited the United States for the first time in 1997 and 1998, to see what Americans turners were doing and to show his work.

Potocnik's multicultural Australian background helps him to understand other cultures, and his travels enable him to better appreciate his own environment. For example, Australia is experiencing a serious extended drought, a problem that has affected Africans for centuries. He explains that travel teaches how good good is, and how bad bad can be.

A weathered old basket standing outside a shop in Katmandu directly inspired his *Doku Bowls*. The round rim tapered to a square bottom. The thirty-inch-tall *doku* basket rested on wooden feet and had a wide strap that went around the forehead so that a farmer could carry it on his back.

Potocnik wanted his bowl to relate closely to the basket, so before he left Nepal, he bought some local asna, a furniture wood that grows in the tropical lowlands of Nepal. He turned a prototype out of scrap and then roughed out a bowl shape in asna. After he carved four square tapering legs on the outside, the bowl just did not feel right. Potocnik removed more and more wood from the interior until he was satisfied with the feel. Finally, he wanted to add a

reference to the original material of the basket—woven bamboo splints. He used a pyrography tool with a knife tip to burn crosshatch cuts on the broad rim.

Inspiration does not always come from a foreign culture. While wandering the streets in Perth one day, he noticed some stylish trash receptacles. The tall metal cylinders were contained in a framework supported on four turned legs that ran up to the broad-brimmed top. What Potocnik saw was a jarrah burl bowl with a beaded ring glued to the rim that would fit into a hole turned in a six-inch square piece of ash. He cut four short legs out of aluminum tubing and turned ebonized wooden caps for the bottom of the feet to suggest bases of

classical columns. Potocnik made several of the bowls, as well as a variation with a round piece of veneered MDF that supported a fiddleback maple bowl. After agonizing about the height, position, and shape of the legs, he settled on four tapered claws. Although earlier versions of this design were up to eighteen-inches square, he finds that smaller pieces are quicker to make and more saleable, too.

Potocnik first explored multi-axis turning, where the wood is mounted off-center, more than ten years ago. He tried several different designs, including his *Sentinel* sculptures, influenced by cairns he had seen marking trails in Nepal. During a conference at Emma Lake in Canada, he collaborated with

Painted Red Gum Boxes, 2007. Red gum; H 1¾" W. 3½" D. 3½". Typical of thousands Potocnik has turned as tourist souvenirs, these boxes are made of Australia's iconic red gum and painted to suggest Aboriginal art.

turner, Merryll Saylan, on another faceted sculpture that was decorated with milk paint and aptly named *Buttermilk Discovered*.

After exploring faceting, Potocnik went on to other things but has come back to it for his *Multi-Axis Boxes*. He cut the three facets on the boxes by mounting the wood on the chuck three different times. The trick is careful measuring, and it took several attempts to get it right. For one he used red gum, a variety of eucalyptus native to

Australia, for the body. He used darker gidgee, a dense wood from the eastern coast of Australia, for the lid. He also turned a gidgee collar for the opening in the box. For the other, he used light-colored canthium for the body and western myall, with a similar grain as gidgee, for the collar.

For flowers growing out of the tops of the boxes, Potocnik acknowledges the inspiration of Michael Mocho, a turner from Albuquerque, whom he met during residency at the Philadelphia Wood Turning Center in 2004. A versatile woodworker, Mocho is best known for combining bent wood with his sculptures. Potocnik refined the concept so that his finial achieves a slender, organic quality complete with three stamens. After he found some steel guitar string that made the perfect filament, he turned tiny teardrop anthers. It was the perfect organic foil for an otherwise rigid form.

Stimulated by his travels, Potocnik is always experimenting. Kenyan and Malawian tourist carving inspired the delicate *Philly Pod* sculptures, slender stems from which pod-like forms hang. He used a variation on the pod form for *Rosewood Evolution*, a series of balls and pods that can be rearranged by the viewer. *Burnt at the Beech* is the shape of a starfish turned from ash and beech and marked with a woodburning tool. The individual S-shaped squiggles can be rearranged at will.

While Potocnik started out turning vessels, he is always exploring the possibilities of many different objects. He makes platters and standard lidded boxes with decidedly non-standard laminated

Rosewood Evolution, 2006. Brazilian rosewood; H. 2" W. 11" D. 5". Presenting Potocnik with a piece of rosewood, a magazine editor asked him to make something and write up the process. The photographer brought a fresh eye and created a beautiful image that Potocnik had not seen in it.

lids and sandblasted and painted surfaces. Cylindrical boxes recall the shape of emperor's hats that he saw on his travels in China. *Rocket Boxes* combined aluminum with his favorite red gum wood.

While Potocnik started out turning vessels, he is always exploring the possibilities of many different objects.

Potocnik has also tried his hand at pure sculpture with a life-size, hand-carved torso that he calls *Defence Shield*. The shape is a response to the "body beautiful" cult that likes to hide behind the perfect shield of their bodies, but they cannot hide what is inside. Other commissions include Torah scrolls for a synagogue and a crucifix and candlesticks for a Lutheran school. He has also designed trophies and awards to honor young artists.

Potocnik sees his life's mission to celebrate wood, which is an integral part of man's environment. He uses the medium to express the ideas he draws from cultures worldwide. Just as wood says something about other cultures, so Potocnik takes these ideas and combines them with his own environment to express new cultural insights.

But the beauty of the natural world humbles him. When he beheld Mt. Everest for the first time, he realized no matter how talented artists are, how beautiful the objects they create, they have no chance to create anything more beautiful than nature.

Elm Burl Box, 2006. Elm burl; H. 8" W. 4" D. 3½".
Elm Burl Box is one of a series of band-sawn boxes. Using a band saw freed Potocnik to explore new shapes and combinations of materials and color.

RICHARD RAFFAN

Born: 1943, Zeal Monachorum, Devon, England

Producing Refined, Simple Shapes

Richard Raffan has taught the world to turn—through his three videos, five books, and more than 450 workshops and demonstrations throughout the world. His titles include *Taunton's Complete Illustrated Guide to Turning*, *Turning Wood* (both of which have sold more than 100,000 copies), *Turning Projects*, *Turning Boxes*, *Turning Bowls*, and *Turned-Bowl Design*, recently revised and reprinted as *The Art of Turned Bowls*.

His first major show was the inaugural British Crafts Council exhibition in 1973. Of 28,000 entries, only 470 were selected, and Raffan was the only turner.

After several false starts, Raffan learned the turning trade the traditional way—by apprenticing. His father was a portrait painter, so in 1962, Raffan decided to study art but dropped out after two years. A stint with a small company that produced Scandinavian-style household goods taught him that it was possible to make something fast and well. Spending the next five years with a wine company, he learned how to manage a business but ultimately found it boring.

Raffan's sister, a potter, suggested he try woodturning. So, on a whim he took her up on the idea and looked for a way to learn the craft. Her studio was located near a production shop run by Douglas Hart, who made bowls, candlesticks, and treenware. Raffan paid Hart

ABOVE
Richard Raffan in his shop at his lathe in Canberra, Australia.

OPPOSITE
Tower Boxes, 2008. French Boxwood.
H. 2" Dia. 1½".
H. 4¾" Dia. 1½".
H. 4" Dia. 1½".
H. 8¾" Dia. 1½".
H. 11½" Dia. 1⅓".

tuition but learned turning primarily by watching his employee, Rendle Crang.

Five months later at age twenty-seven, he set out on his own and started experimenting with different woods and tools. He turned bowls, table lamps, and sugar bowls with scoops. During his career, he has turned 24,000 scoops and even more bowls. At first, he sold everything out of the back of his car to craft shops in the area, but soon orders were coming directly to him through word-of-mouth and repeat customers.

Ceramics influenced his bowls from the very beginning, when he was a member of the Devon Guild of Craftsmen. The membership included many distinguished potters, notably Bernard Leach and his family. Japanese and Korean rice bowls that he saw at the Victorian Arts Center in Melbourne also impressed him. Although he likes the rice bowl form, he often turns

his bowls with green wood so they will twist and warp as the wood dries. Boxes, however, require dry wood so that the lid will fit properly.

His first major show was the inaugural British Crafts Council exhibition in 1973. Of 28,000 entries, only 470 were selected, and Raffan was the only turner. This led to invitations to a number of other high-profile craft exhibitions during the 1970s, and his career took off.

Raffan performed his first public demonstration in 1981 at the first international turning symposium in Britain, sponsored by John Makepeace, the founder of the School for Craftsmen in Wood at Parnham House. Makepeace insisted Raffan demonstrate after he had been characteristically blunt about the sad state of the turning he had seen at a show of Worshipful Company of Turners in London. Makepeace hoped to improve the

All photos by Richard Raffan.

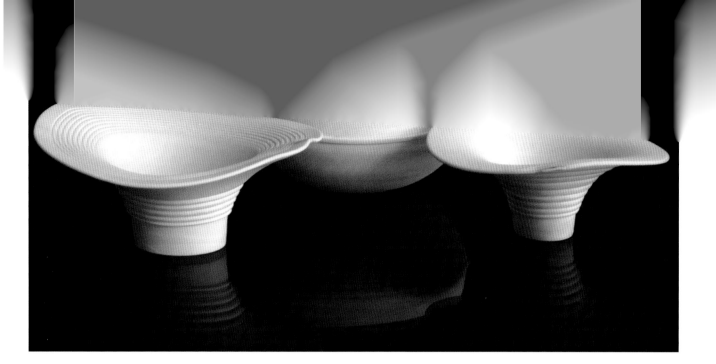

situation by gathering together some of the most renowned turners of the time.

At the conference, David Ellsworth from the United States made Raffan aware of Albert LeCoff's turning conferences in Philadelphia, and the next year he won a grant to attend. Contacts there led to

Buildings have always inspired Raffan, and he might have become an architect if he had been better at math and physics.

requests from Dale Nish at Brigham Young University in Provo, Utah, to demonstrate at his woodturning conferences.

After that, the invitations never ceased, even though he emigrated from England to Australia in 1982 where he had extensive family connections and where he had lived in the late-1940s. Several years before emigrating, he had served as a craftsman-in-residence at the Sturt Workshops, a center for craft production and education south of Sydney. He now works in Canberra from a small shed in his backyard.

Raffan's *Tower Boxes* were inspired by photographs of Indian burial pyres he saw in Sydney in the late-1990s. Variations on this theme, also suggestive of mosque minarets or cathedral spires, have been among his signature designs since the late-1970s. Buildings have always inspired Raffan, and he might have become an architect if he had been better at math and physics. His forms sometimes echo architectural masterpieces but more often recall humble structures such as African grain stores, European pigeon lofts, or farmers' haystacks.

He likes to turn clusters of boxes so that the village can be rearranged at will. The smallest box in *Tower Boxes*, he explains, is like a pretender or the baby of the family. Although it takes a long time to dry, the tightly grained French boxwood is stable and ideal for turning slender boxes that must fit together with close tolerances.

The uninitiated might wonder how hard it could be to turn a snugly fitting lid—surely just a matter of turning one cylinder to slide over the other. The problem is that lids

Wavy Bowls; 2008. Holly; Dia. 3½" to 4". Raffan likes to use holly because it deforms into interesting shapes after he hastens drying in a microwave.

Bowl, 2008. Madrone burl; Dia. 7½". As with most of his bowls, Raffan turned the wood green and left it unsanded. As with holly, madrone warps unpredictably when drying.

Boxes, 2008. Left: Australian dead finish; Dia. 2⅜". Right: Tasmanian horizontal scrub; Dia. 2¹⁵⁄₁₆". Usually box blanks are cut well clear of the pith, but Tasmanian horizontal scrub has solid pith that rarely splits, so boxes can be turned from whole logs that offer striking grain patterns.

tend to be too loose, or else fit so tightly that they will not come off easily. A groove in the cylinder would allow the air to escape and unstick the lid, but it is unsightly. Raffan developed a better way that achieves the soft-suction fit for which he is famous. The flange on the base is turned slightly convex so that the lid slips off easily with a pleasing pop. The idea is simple, but the skill required is not. Raffan admits his students will ruin more than a few boxes before perfecting the technique.

The boxes are turned smooth both inside and out, sanded with abrasive up to 800 grit, and then finished with linseed oil and beeswax. He avoids high gloss lacquer or varnish because he wants his work to be handled, and handling will degrade the finishes. Some of his bowls are ebonized with a stain made of rusty nails in vinegar and others have a verdigris finish. He likes to fool people into thinking they are picking up metal bowls. It is all part of his crusade to force people to appreciate the workmanship and form before they rhapsodize about the material or the finish.

Ten years ago, Raffan turned his first *Citadel Boxes* out of degraded burl. They were cylindrical like his *Stacks* and *Pipes* but had onion-shaped lids. The shape evokes fortress towers or the profile of Victorian fire hydrants. With only a four-inch-deep storage space, these foot-tall boxes are quite heavy and useful for holding maybe a single ring. He has never liked large hollow vessels, which, he says, are more appropriate in ceramic or glass. Deep cavities in wooden containers serve no real functional purpose, he declares. Although it takes a high degree of skill to hollow a vessel, he points out that a number of new tools are available and the techniques are so well-known that hollowing can be about as monotonous as turning pens.

After turning the cylinders, he scored the façade with a Dremel tool, burned the surface with a torch, and then abraded the charred wood with a rotating wire brush. In fact, these boxes demonstrate Raffan's critiques of the turning field. They are a vivid personal statement against ever smoother and shinier surfaces and the common preoccupation with finish. *Citadel Boxes* stand in direct contrast to his highly refined and finely crafted *Tower Boxes*.

In the mid-1970s, he sold several hundred boxes annually but now maybe half that number. Boxes represent only about five percent of his total output, with bowls by far his major focus. Little of his work is available in the United States because he can sell everything he makes wholesale for immediate cash while American galleries typically take only consignments.

Today, he does more teaching than turning, but even after almost forty years of experience, Raffan still strives to produce ever more refined and simpler shapes. He sums up his work by declaring, "I don't feel the need to be different, but I would like to be good."

Very good, indeed.

ABOVE TOP

Stacks and *Pipes*, 2005. Oak; H. 14" Dia. 1" to 3". Raffan cuts grooves in his stacks and leaves the pipes smooth.

ABOVE BOTTOM

Box, 2007. Eucalyptus burl; Dia. 6". Like a medieval tower, this box has a lid turned with steps to suggest a roof. Like all of his boxes, these have Raffan's signature suction-fit lids.

ULRIKE SCRIBA

Born: 1944, Worms, Germany

Modern Designs, Traditional Techniques

Ulrike Scriba is following in the tradition of the famous eighteenth century German cabinetmakers such as Abraham and David Roentgen, Jean-Francois Oeben, and Jean-Henri Riesener, who produced some of the most extraordinary marquetry furniture ever made. When many of these German-born cabinetmakers

---

Following the eighteenth century tradition, Scriba cuts marquetry by hand. It is a dying or maybe a dead art because it is so costly and time-consuming.

---

were enticed to work for the French court at Versailles, they turned their talents to decorating cabinets and desks with perspective scenes and floral decoration that were enjoyed by the king. The *Bureau du Roi*, for Louis XV, was begun by Oeben in 1760 and completed by Riesener nine years later.

Growing up in Darmstadt, Scriba was surrounded by art, particularly German Art Nouveau, from the *Jugenstil* that thrived there in the 1890s. But despite her immersion in art, she had no idea she would eventually dedicate her life to keeping the noble craft of German marquetry alive. She had been exposed to the crafts at a young age because her father earned a living producing brass and copper items to sell. Scriba often worked in her father's shop and made her first wood and metal crafts as a teenager. In 1961, she enrolled in sculpture classes at the School of Arts and Crafts in Darmstadt.

Photo by Ulrike Scriba.

ABOVE

Ulrike Scriba carving with her grandson, Ajaya, in her studio in Gengenbach, Germany.

OPPOSITE

Box, 2008. Walnut, ebony, and silver; H. 4⅓" W. 2⅓" D. 2⅓".

But with no clear direction, she left school after three years to take a job working on the restoration of the Weurzburg Residence in Bavaria.

This 300-room Baroque sandstone palace, designed by renowned German architect, Balthasar Neumann, took twenty-two years to build in the early eighteenth century. It was badly damaged during World War II, but fortunately, much of the interior woodwork and furnishings had been photographed and removed for safekeeping. Scriba spent five years restoring the stucco walls and ceilings, and became involved with the furniture conservation that was also part of the project.

In 1969, Scriba left to marry and start a family. Her husband was a ceramicist, and she initially helped him in his studio, but she wanted her own shop. She decided to start an antique restoration business specializing in the repair of old veneer. The workshop is located in her home surrounded by vineyards in Gengenbach, in Germany's Black Forest region not far from Strassburg in France. She started to construct her own marquetry tables, and by 1976, was making her first boxes.

With no one to help her, Scriba taught herself marquetry techniques through trial and error. She still relishes the "aha!" moments that led her to new insights. She feels fortunate to be self-trained, like her father, because she has not been constrained by a rigid traditional art education. She has learned much from other crafts. Bookbinding techniques, for example, have improved her process for gluing up veneers.

Following the eighteenth century tradition, Scriba cuts marquetry by hand.

Jewelry Box, 2000. Lebanon Cedar, wengé; H. 3" W. 17" D. 17". Scriba is best known for marquetry boxes, but she also has made a few jewelry boxes out of solid wood. The fragrance of the cedar and the addition of a secret compartment add interest.

Photos by Paul Clemens.

It is a dying or maybe a dead art because it is so costly and time-consuming. What marquetry there is today is mostly laser-cut by computer-controlled tools. She does it the old-fashioned way by stacking up to eight sheets of different woods, drawing a design on the top sheet, and then cutting patterns in the stack with a fine scroll saw. Then the individual pieces of wood from the different sheets are mixed and combined to reproduce the same pattern but with different woods, a process much like working a jigsaw puzzle. The pieces are glued to a backing, then pairs of sheets are stacked again to be cut into new patterns that are then mixed and glued up again. The process can be repeated up to three times before the individual pieces become too small to handle. Although Scriba tries to imagine the result during the design stage, the finished product always provides a few surprises. Sometimes the result is flawed, and she has to start all over again.

Early in her career, she experimented with a dizzying variety of woods, packing in as many exotics as possible, but she soon realized less was more. Scriba also discovered local species such as bog oak found in the gravel pits along the Danube and the Main rivers. This wood runs from

Scriba does not try to imitate the old marquetry masters nor copy a false Baroque style, but rather, she revives the craft to produce her own contemporary designs.

grey to black and is a good substitute for ebony. She also likes lacewood and European walnut burl, which she gets from across the French border in Lorraine.

Initially, Scriba created simple abstract patterns suggesting flowers, leaves or regular

Untitled box with silver lid, 2004. European walnut, sapeli-pommele, sterling silver; H. 3¾" W. 3⅓" D. 3⅓". Each wood has its own color and figure, but when combined into infinite marquetry patterns, the effect is fresh and intense.

This silver lid (inset) shows the embossed pattern that repeats the marquetry on the box sides.

Cube Box, 2003.
Bubinga, bog oak, koto;
H. 4" W. 4¾" D. 4¾"
The decoration on
Cube Box suggests
an interesting textile.
Scriba cuts a textured
pattern into the
bubinga to expose
the marquetry below,
like the sgraffito
(scratched) technique
in ceramics.

The surface of *Cube Box*
(inset) shows the linear
textured pattern.

geometrical designs, such as chevrons or checkers. She glued these thin marquetry sheets onto the outside and inside of cube-shaped boxes made of plywood, onto shallow trays, and sometimes onto pyramids. She also experimented with irregularly shaped boxes made out of veneered plywood. After a visit to the city of Nancy, France, home of renown Art Nouveau designers Louis Majorelle and Emile Gallé, her work became more complex. She was particularly impressed with the inlaid furniture she saw there.

Her trays and wall hangings have a greater range of designs. Some of the marquetry repeats a zigzag pattern or is made up of odd shapes that could have come from a Joan Miró painting or an Alexander Calder mobile. A group of wall hangings with a series of intersecting straight lines look convincingly like loosely woven cloth. Unlike eighteenth century marquetry, which was mostly pictorial, Ulrike's designs often suggest textiles. She sometimes combines similarly colored woods with different grain pattern to give the illusion of some strange exotic wood. Other times the pattern is clearly delineated with light and dark woods.

Her later boxes, made with solid quarter-inch thick marquetry rather than veneered plywood, feature slightly bowed sides. The curves are hand-shaped like a piece of sculpture. The mitered corners are glued together, and a rabbeted bottom board is glued on. An inner liner projects slightly above the body of the box to hold the lid in place. She applies Danish oil, polished using the lathe as a buffer and then a final coat of lanolin wax.

Scriba is always open to experimentation. Several years ago, a German woodworking supply firm, gave her a roll of fish skin. She covered part of a box with it—the light colored, pebbly skin creating an interesting contrast with dark, smooth ebony, and walnut.

Scriba's boxes have something the eighteenth century master marquetarians did not conceive. While the finest French cabinets were fitted with cast ormolu metal mounts, Scriba has embellished her boxes with silver lids. Because Scriba grew up in her father's metal working shop, metalworking was familiar to her. When she took a silversmithing workshop in 2001, the metalsmithing techniques quickly came back to her.

She passes a sheet of silver through rollers to emboss it with the same marquetry pattern that is on the sides of the box. She then forms the silver sheet around a wooden lid. She performs the silver work in the studio of her nephew, a professional silversmith, but it is nearly 200 miles away, so she hopes one day to have her own silver studio.

Scriba does not try to imitate the old marquetry masters nor copy a false Baroque style, but rather, she is happy to revive the craft and use it to produce her own contemporary designs. In this fast-paced modern world, it is fortunate she has the patience to fit tiny pieces of wood together into ever more complex patterns that delight our senses and keep alive an ancient and awe-inspiring craft.

Small Chest of Drawers, 2006. Burl birch, maple, cherry, wild service tree; H. 2¾" W. 10¼" D. 5½". Most of Ulrike's boxes have a lift-off lid, but this box is equipped with a drawer.

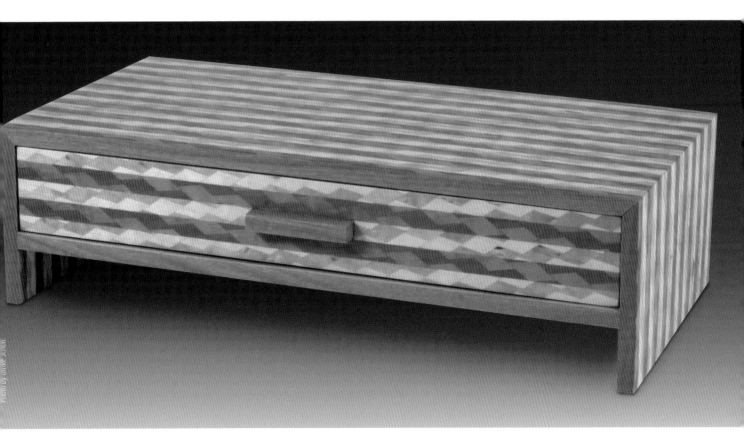

Jeff and Katrina Seaton

(Jeff) Born: 1947, Buffalo, New York
(Katrina) Born: 1953, Los Angeles, California

Teamwork Creates Boxes That Are Right

Jeff Seaton's mother was an artist, and when he was a child, he helped her make a workbench and desk for his bedroom. Although he took woodshop in school and built model airplanes and cars, woodworking did not capture his attention until 1973. He had been working construction jobs in Mendocino, California, when he

Another person who encouraged him was legendary woodturner Bob Stocksdale, who was impressed with what he saw and reinforced the idea that Seaton should just keep making what he liked.

cut open a huge redwood burl and, overwhelmed by its color and figure, just had to do something special with it. He gets the same feeling every time he cuts into a piece of wood and reveals the beauty of nature.

Although he started out to make big furniture with the burl, Seaton quickly realized it was easier to make little boxes. He soon discovered other woods like bird's-eye maple and mountain lilac burl that grow in Southern California. It was a short jump to imported exotic woods.

During the past twenty years, he has purchased hardwood from a dealer whose family lives in Mexico. Oxen that pull dead trees to the sawmill harvest most of the wood. Part of the profits goes to buy fencing to keep cattle out of the forest so that new growth can flourish.

Photo by Michael Hamilton.

ABOVE

Jeff and Katrina Seaton at Cedar Breaks National Monument in Utah. Mountain biking is the couple's way of relaxing after their grueling craft show schedule.

OPPOSITE

Mirrored Images, 2008. Australian lacewood, cocobolo, maple, ebony, black palm, Russian masur birch, Cambodian amboyna burl; H. 14" W. 6" D. 6".

Elliptical Monoliths, Nesting Set, 2006. Cocobolo, rosewood; H. 15" W. 7" D. 7". The couple's most challenging design, all three boxes in the set are band sawn out of a single block of rosewood. Shaker oval boxes and nesting boxes from Russia inspired the nesting boxes.

His favorite wood is cocobolo, a rosewood from Mexico and Central America.

Seaton is largely self-taught, with help from some friends and co-workers during his early years in Mendocino. He also read the books by James Krenov, who taught at the College of the Redwoods in nearby Fort Bragg, and learned from some of his students. From them he gained a respect for the wood and for traditional cabinetmaking techniques.

Another person who encouraged him was Bob Stocksdale, the legendary woodturner. In 1981, Seaton was showing at a craft fair in San Francisco when Stocksdale came into his booth. The master was impressed with what he saw and reinforced the idea that Seaton should just keep making what he liked. Following that advice to this day, Seaton has found that if he likes a piece, people will buy it. As a result, he rarely accepts commissions other than a few cremation urns. Stocksdale also invited him to his studio in Berkeley for a turning lesson. After that, Jeff went through a period of turning knobs for handles that pierced the top of his boxes and locked the lids.

Seaton sells his boxes at twenty or so galleries around the country, and at a half-dozen craft shows each year. Most of his production boxes measure about three inches tall and five inches square, or come in a rectangular three-by-five-by-twelve-inch size. The majority are band sawn from blocks of African bubinga, the technique pioneered by Art Carpenter, who worked in northern California from about 1950 until his death in 2006.

Seaton used to cut the box bottom out of the wood sawn from the interior of the box, but he now uses a slice of particle board instead, because it is more stable. He saws the particle board about a sixteenth of an inch narrower than the width of the box, then glues leather on both sides.

Of the 400 boxes he makes each year, only about ten are signature models with fancy designs and premium woods. For the past few years he has also experimented with applying patinated, copper repoussé panels to the front surface. One plate, for example, suggested birds, while other patterns on the copper were drawn from ancient Southwest Indian petroglyphs that the couple discovered on their travels in that part of the country. He has also experimented with raffia that he saw on Santa Fe Indian crafts. Objects from nature such as leaves, birds, horses, or fish also inspire the work.

Seaton believes all wood has a history, so the challenge is to capture that story.

More recently, Seaton has focused on the wood grain and the effects he can achieve from book-matching and similar techniques. He recognizes all wood has a history, so the challenge is to capture that story. "Some," he says, "tell their story visually, others tactilely, or aromatically. Still others, like the extremely rare African pink ivory wood, are themselves the source of myth and legend in their native homeland."

Lacewood Chest, 2007. Australian lacewood, curly big leaf maple, ebony; H. 6" W. 11" D. 7". Selecting only the most unusual hardwoods, the Seatons let the woods tell their story. For *Lacewood Chest,* the maple body and the ebony accents set off the Australian lacewood.

Living with Your Flaws, 1989. Hawaiian Koa; H. 5" W. 20" D. 12". Typical of Seaton's early work, *Living with Your Flaws* was cut from a single block of wood with striking figure. As exotic woods have gotten harder to find, Seaton is using more veneers.

His machinery—an eight-inch jointer, a fifteen-inch surface planer, and a twelve-inch disc sander—limits the dimensions of his boxes. But within those parameters the particular species and grain of the wood determines the size. For *Mirrored Images* he selected seven different exotic woods and added a low cherry platform. In contrast to his typically horizontal production boxes, he orients his signature work vertically, like pieces of sculpture.

The focus of *Mirrored Images* is on a double booked-matched cocobolo panel pegged and glued to the front. It suggests a tunnel. The cocobolo is framed with ebony and enhanced with maple steps. He repeated the step effect on the arches, which are capped with black palm. The arch shape, repeated on the lid, serves as a handle. The lid is also decorated with the maple step motif and further embellished with a mottled, oyster-shell pattern made of Russian masur birch with eight, yellowish Cambodian amboyna

cubes. Instead of a hinged lid, Seaton prefers a lift-off top so the customer can experience the smoothness of the wood. His intricate lid patterns have inspired him lately to experiment with adapting them for wall hangings.

The last step is finishing. He built his own disc sander with interchangeable pads so that he can efficiently sand the box with seven different grits from forty to 600. Then he applies a Danish oil finish and uses a buffing wheel and carnauba wax for the final polish. Customers always respond to the silky soft feel. Lately, he has been experimenting with urethane varnish to better seal the wood.

Seaton worked from a shop in an industrial park in Santa Barbara until about fifteen years ago when he moved to Ojai, California, where he and his wife, Katrina, share a shop. It is a pleasant fifty-yard commute from their house. Although Ojai is a quaint rural town with a large artist community, Seaton's work keeps him from participating as much as he would like. While Santa Barbara is known for its scenic beauty, Ojai is more rural—he is close to nature, which has always influenced his work.

After he married Katrina in 1984, Seaton says his boxes improved. She runs the office and helps with the finishing, including the leather and copper work. She is also a glass artist with a refined sense of color. He tries out his ideas on her "like a second head." She is always right, and so are their boxes.

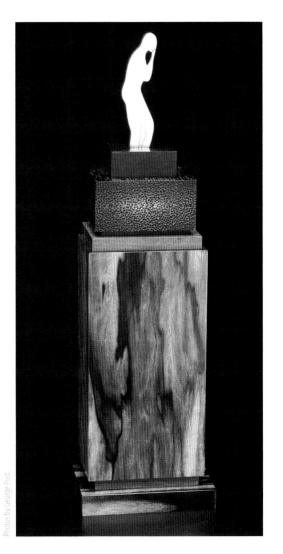

ABOVE

Flying Fish, 2004. Ebony, cocobolo, maple, Hawaiian koa, satine, copper, silver, gold-plated hardware; H. 15" W. 8" D. 8". *Flying Fish* features Katrina Seaton's copper repoussé work. People frequently note a Japanese influence in the couple's work.

LEFT

Sorrows, 1995. Macassar ebony, copper, black palm; H. 17" W. 7" D. 5". Seaton created *Sorrows* while mourning the loss of a close friend. The figure is a silhouette cut out of copper and laminated onto a piece of ebony.

TOMMY SIMPSON

Born: 1939, Elgin, Illinois

Reaching Viewers through Universal Symbols

Tommy Simpson has made objects and paintings ever since he was a child in Dundee, Illinois. Growing up in the safety of this small Midwestern town, he had the freedom to develop and explore the world on his own terms: walking to school, camping, canoeing, building soap-box racers, and nursing wounded birds back to

"The art of making brings to me a joyful awareness of my body, heart, and mind," Simpson says.

health. At age six, his great aunt Florence taught him to paint flowers.

His father, a doctor, hoped Simpson would follow his example. However, when he went off to the University of Illinois, he deliberately failed his pre-med examinations, freeing him to explore the career of an artist. Along the way, he traveled to Hawaii and Europe, and attended four other universities. He explored pottery and fine art. By 1964, he received a master's degree in painting and printmaking from the Cranbrook Academy of Art, and embraced the life of the artist he was always meant to become.

Since then, Simpson has experimented with almost every medium of art including painting, furniture, sculpture, textiles, and even porcelain, red-ware, and enameled jewelry. He also discovered a talent for writing with his first book, *Fantasy Furniture*, which was followed by two more books, *Hand and Home*, and his

Photo by Karen LaFleur

ABOVE

Tommy Simpson having tea with a teddy bear in his studio in Milford, Connecticut.

OPPOSITE

Tooling Tennessee Box, 1994. Basswood, iron, and acrylic paint; H. 18" W. 24" D. 10".

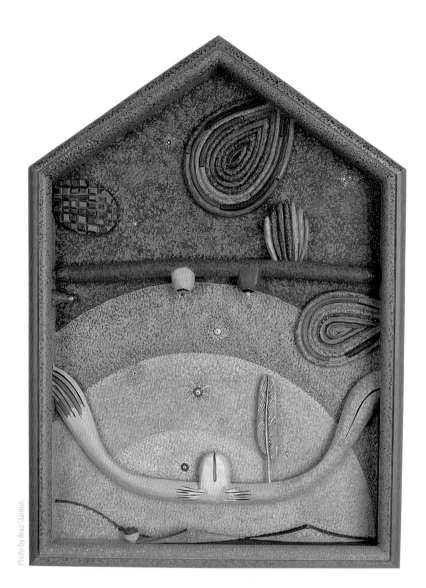

*House of Midnight Wants,*1998. Painted wood; H. 27" W. 19½" D. 2¼". Simpson explains *House of Midnight Wants:* "Our desires take on different shades of blue, especially when the sun does its evening retreat."

gouache paintings, toy-like objects, and humorous narrative sculptures similar to H. C. Westermann's art. Many pieces include historical references and found objects like buttons, brushes, tools, and feathers. Recently, he also has explored designs for wool rugs.

Most of Simpson's art is autobiographical, but the experiences he relates have universal appeal. For example, his *G. W. Cabinet,* now in the Renwick collection of the Smithsonian American Art Museum, recalls the time in sixth grade when he was cast as George Washington in the school play. It was an uncomfortable role for a child who had not experienced standing in front of a crowd. And to make matters worse, his pants ripped as he took his final bows. Who has not had similar embarrassing moments?

As an artist, Simpson often uses his furniture as a large canvas. That is why he prefers bigger cabinets and armoires to small boxes. However, when he was teaching a workshop, he wanted a small demonstration piece that he could easily take home—hence the toolbox. The painting tools determined the size of the box he planned to carry. He has saved it ever since for his daughter, who asked to inherit it someday.

After returning home to Connecticut, Simpson made the iron handle. He forged the metal part of the handle out of square stock to fit into the turned wooden handle. Painted metal strips nailed to the box top's edges ensure the handle will not break under a load. To keep the lid in place, he cut the lid slightly shorter than the ends of the box. Then he glued a row of bristles from a brush to each end of the lid. Pushing down

autobiographical *Two Looks to Home.* The urge to create dominates his life. "The art of making brings to me a joyful awareness of my body, heart, and mind," he says.

Unfettered by a traditional cabinetmaking background, Simpson first produced organic-shaped furniture with brightly colored characters and abstract decoration. Gesso covered up simple peg construction and provided a canvas he could enrich with carving and paint. His early work has been compared to ceramics by Peter Voulkos. Both craftsmen broke with traditional forms and techniques and explored the possibilities of their medium by expressing meaning beyond mere function. Simpson gradually expanded his repertoire to include small on the lid bends the bristles and secures the lid in place. The corners are mitered and glued so that no joints interfere with the carving. The ball feet are attached with dowel-screws that have opposing threads on either end.

The surface decoration is typical of Simpson's work. It usually suggests a landscape, cityscape, or seascape. He purposely keeps the composition understated, so viewers can form their own

As an artist, Simpson often uses his furniture as a large canvas. That is why he prefers bigger cabinets and armoires to small boxes.

interpretations. Pablo Picasso once observed artists take a lifetime to relearn how to be as spontaneous as children. Simpson's artwork certainly captures the spirit of childlike spontaneity.

For him, carving and painting are the same. He used various gouges to cut the textures on the toolbox façade and then covered the surface with gesso and paint. In the blue area, he applied a second coat of green with a rubber roller to highlight the cut-marks. Knowing his childhood, it is easy to imagine the blue referring to the Fox River that flowed through his hometown, and the furrowed red areas as plowed fields.

For the viewer, Simpson's art speaks in universal symbols that everyone can relate to. The black handhold on the lid could be a whale, while other shapes are fish in the sea. The swirling splotch of color in the water suggests a hurricane tracking toward landfall, or maybe the land itself is slowly

Photo by Brad Stanton.

Souperman, 2004. Mixed wood; H. 74" W. 33" D. 18". "I'm not allowed to tell you about the *Souperman*," whispers Simpson. "His souper-powers are secret."

The Four Rivers, 2004. Mixed wood; H. 72" W. 32" D. 19". *The Four Rivers* is based on an ancient Persian garden divided into quarters representing the four seasons, the four heavens, and the four winds. Called a "parades," it gave rise to our word paradise.

Photo by Brad Stanton.

falling into the sea. A flower drifts over the water dropping its petals in the ocean. The smooth balls that carry the box contrast with the lively design, suggesting an oasis of stability in an inherently unstable world. About all that is missing from the toolbox are the birds and people that frequently populate his other landscapes.

Simpson refers to his artwork as "abstract narratives" that are really manifestations of his own inner world. Working in the studio adjacent to his house in the small town of New Milford, Connecticut, Simpson keeps alive the values of a bygone era when children were free to test themselves and explore the world. As we enjoy his universe, we are reminded of our own childhood and the lessons we learned from our family, our friends, and our neighborhoods.

ABOVE

Carpenter's Chair, 1991. Mixed wood; H. 56" W. 36"
D. 24". *Carpenter's Chair* pays homage to the Shaker
craftsmen who in their search for simplicity gave
the world many wonderful designs.

RIGHT

Night Rambler, 2004. Painted wood; H. 81" W. 27"
D. 15". Simpson painted the cabinet of *Night
Rambler* white, varnished it, and then applied
a mixture of glazes with black pigment that he
scratched through to reveal the white undercoat.
The effect is much like children's finger painting.

BONNIE KLEIN
JACQUES VESERY

(Bonnie) Born: 1942, Los Angeles, California
(Jacques) Born: 1960, Westwood, New Jersey

Creating Containers of Stories

Jacques Vesery is a sculptor, not a box maker. Bonnie Klein is famous for her spin top boxes. Together, they have produced some exquisite collaborations that would rival Fabergé eggs if Carl Fabergé had ever worked in wood. In fact, *The Birth of a Fabergé Wanna Be*, a gilt-trimmed spin-top box emerging from a cracked egg, was

---

With her portable lathe and thread-cutting jig, Klein traveled all over the country and became famous for her spin-top boxes.

---

one of their first joint projects. Their collaborations produce art in the tradition of precious *objects de virtue*, confections of craft skills that can be used as containers but are mainly designed to be admired. Collaborations are not unique to the turning field, but they may be more pervasive in this traditionally close-knit profession than others. Michael Hosaluk's (see page 85) Emma Lake conferences in Canada certainly have fostered this way of working.

Because her father was a builder, Klein grew up around wood and tools. After studying at the University of Hawaii, she married a Navy man and started a family in Renton, Washington, near Seattle. When her daughter wanted a dollhouse, she bought a Shopsmith and built one in the studio behind her house where she still works. In the early 1980s, she became interested in small tools and turning and began attending the turning symposiums in Utah as well as the annual

ABOVE TOP

Jacques Vesery with some of his work outside in Damariscotta, Maine.

ABOVE BOTTOM

Bonnie Klein at her home in Renton, Washington.

OPPOSITE

As the World Turns & the Seasons Spin, 2009. Swiss pear, white oak, mammoth ivory, silver and gold leaf; H. 6" W. 21" D. 5".

The Birth of a Fabergé
Wanna Be, 2002. Maple,
holly, madrone, walnut,
gold leaf; H. 7" Dia. 5".
Vesery made The Birth
of a Fabergé Wanna
Be in collaboration
with Klein after an
exhibition review said
his work had traits of
a Fabergé egg.

Vesery. Klein turned four identical spin-top boxes with thick sides and handles that Vesery could carve. Winter is covered in lichen-encrusted bark, ice, and snow. Spring turns blue enveloped in feathers with a pile of sticks to make a bird's nest. A yellow day lily blooms in summer, while fall features oak leaves with a few tiny acorns. Each box contains a tiny turned surprise: a snowman for winter, an egg for spring, an ice-cream cone for summer, and an acorn for fall.

The color schemes inside the boxes reinforce the theme. Winter's interior features a cold blue night sky. During spring, the sky turns light blue with clouds, and in summer, a yellowish haze sets in, while the fall sky takes on the hue of a sunset. For the exterior of winter alone, the application of seven different layers of white, black, blue, purple, and off-white to achieve the translucent depth of the snow and bark took longer than carving the feathers on spring. The turned gilt or silvered beads tie the four seasons together. The four spin tops rest on magnets embedded in the square bases attached to the white oak stands.

Like Klein, Vesery was always making things. When he was three years old, his father caught him trying to chop down an ornamental tree with a plastic hatchet. His father had a small shop in the basement and ran a machinist business servicing printing companies. Vesery turned his first wood on a metal lathe even before taking woodworking classes in school.

Fresh out of high school he joined the U.S. Navy to become a pilot, but they needed submariners so he did that for four

American Association of Woodworkers (AAW) meetings.

Recognizing the need for a small portable lathe, in 1986, she began to design and manufacture a line of tools to fill that demand. Several years later, she developed a jig that could cut threads on a box and its lid. With her portable lathe and thread-cutting jig, she traveled all over the country demonstrating and selling her tools. She became famous for her spin-top boxes. With a long handle and a pointed foot, the box could be spun like a top by twisting the handle between thumb and finger.

As the World Turns & the Seasons Spin is the ninth collaboration between Klein and years. Mustered out in Hawaii, he turned his navigation skills to piloting a Zamboni ice-surfacing machine for a year before moving back to the mainland and taking a job demonstrating scrimshaw carving. He had started carving in Hawaii, using a kit he ordered from Mystic Seaport Museum in Connecticut.

Vesery got a job as a ranger managing a 186-acre Boy Scout camp in New Jersey, near where he grew up. About 1987, one of his former high school teachers was cleaning out the wood shop and gave the camp a 1928 Oliver lathe. Vesery got it working, and in his spare time refined his turning skills.

In 1990, he relocated to Maine with his new wife, Minda Gold, who had accepted a medical residency in Portland. At the end of her residency, they moved to Damariscotta, where she started a family practice. He became the stay-at-home dad for their two sons and decided to make furniture in a shop next to his home situated on a three-acre wooded lot just

ABOVE

National Treasures, 2008. Historic woods, steel; H. 8" Dia. 5". Vesery and Klein collaborated to make *National Treasures*, an elaborate top, for the annual American Association of Woodturners (AAW) auction in Richmond, Virginia. It uses wood from four historic Virginia sites, including Mount Vernon.

LEFT

National Treasures (detail). The many monuments around Richmond and the state inspired the carving details. Inside the top and on the bottom are maps of Virginia.

As the World Turns Green with Envy of the Sun and Moon, 2007. Cherry, pear, koa, glass; H. 6" Dia. 4". Following the 2006 AAW auction, Vesery believed he and Klein could not top the baseball piece, but then on his way home, he sketched this idea for the next auction. It raised record-breaking funds for the AAW education fund.

beautiful wood was not the most important goal. Instead, he started to color and texture his work in a unique style, and almost overnight, he achieved national recognition.

In 1998, he exhibited at the AAW symposium in Cleveland, and was featured in an article in *American Woodturner* the next year. He could not make work fast enough. He roughs out his design with a rotary tool and then carves the fine details with a sharp-edged woodburning tool. It is a heated knife that he can control with precision.

He paints the scorched surface with India ink and then applies up to seven thin coats of paint in different shades to enhance the texture. He enjoys the contrast between light and dark, rough and smooth. His use of color is informed by the Impressionist painters who believed that forms were more effectively expressed by color than by line.

Although Vesery's style is easily recognizable, it is expressed in myriad designs. He clearly prefers the circle to the square because, he observes, the latter flows while the former catches. The circle theme is evident in his standard footed vessels and bowls, which he calls his *Classic Forms*, and in his *Diversity in the Round Series*, all turned from single pieces of cherry. These include *That's a Wrap*, a turned ball wrapped with rope; *Roll Away the Dew*, suggesting a cantaloupe; and *Junkyard Dog Ball*, wound with scrap metal and fastened with nuts and bolts—all carved in wood. His almost round *Spirit Stones* look just like stones but with feathers carved in them like rare geodes.

His *Pleiades Series*, named for the Seven Sisters constellation, takes the shape of acorns with different leaf, feather, and bark

outside of town. His clean, well-lit studio feels like a shipshape submarine.

Soon, he recognized that small turnings sold better than furniture, and he began to offer his skills to other woodworkers. After a couple of years of mostly working for others, he wanted to concentrate on his own work. Vesery came to the realization that focusing on material and featuring

textures, and gilded interiors. He named the first one *Flight of the Missing Seventh Sister*, a reference to disappearing starlight caused by worldwide ambient nighttime illumination.

His *Seaforms* evolved the idea further. While looking at his standard vessels, one night he got the idea of cutting different shaped openings in them. Two or three

---

Although Vesery's style is easily recognizable, it is expressed in myriad designs.

---

inches long, the sculptures display textured shell-like forms juxtaposed with natural materials such as a carved opal or a piece of amber. The surfaces evoke tree bark (*Hidden between Bark and Light*), woven splint (*The Enigma from Within*), coffee beans (*Coffee Break at Sea*), or coral (*Pebbles to a Sea's Stone*).

Although not a tea drinker, he could not resist the challenge of a teapot competition. Now he makes a teapot almost every year. He is not a baseball fan either, but in 2006, he agreed to create a piece for an exhibit at the Louisville Slugger Museum in Kentucky.

This project led to an intricate sculpture complete with leather glove, ball and bat, and a top that opens up to a tiny baseball diamond.

Thriving on challenges, Vesery has taken Klein's iconic spin-top boxes and enlivened them with stories. As realistic as his carving and coloring is, his intent is to create an illusion of reality, not to duplicate nature. The boxes are containers, yes, but also containers of stories—stories, like art, that people can interpret on their own and that can provoke them to look at nature and themselves in a new way.

ABOVE

'Put me in coach, I'm ready to top that,' 2006. Cherry, holly, maple; H. 6" Dia. 5". Klein turned and Vesery carved and painted *'Put me in coach, I'm ready to top that'* for a baseball exhibit at the Louisville Slugger Museum.

ABOVE LEFT

Put me in coach, I'm ready to top that' (detail). A baseball sails through the clouds on its way out of the park.

PHILIP WEBER
Born: 1952, New York City, New York

Crafting Heirlooms from Raw Wood

When he was a child growing up in New York City, Philip Weber never imagined making a living as a box maker but that is just what he does—and does well. Unlike Frank Lloyd Wright's mother, who plied her young son with building blocks, Weber's parents innocently gave their children the usual 1950s assortment of leather wallet kits, paint-by-number sets, and mosaic tiles. Little did they know that this early exposure to craft would lead to a career.

Weber realized after a couple of years of college that the academic life was not for him and enrolled in a farrier school to learn how to make horseshoes and shoe horses. He liked the making part, but gave up horseshoes in 1976 to start a small craft business, selling boxes and other small items at local craft shows. After he got married, Weber moved to North Carolina where he began working in a small factory that manufactured garden furniture.

Weber's early boxes reflected the ideas of James Krenov, which he absorbed through reading the woodworking books the master craftsman published in the 1970s.

In 1982, just after his daughter was born, he decided to go back to boxes and has been making them ever since. Weber's early boxes reflected the ideas of James Krenov, which he absorbed though reading the woodworking books the master craftsman published

ABOVE

Philip Weber in his studio in Effort, Pennsylvania, during Summer 2008.

OPPOSITE

Oval Exploration, 2008. Ebony, holly, sterling silver; H. 3⅞" W. 8⅜" D. 3⅜".

in the 1970s. Impressed with Krenov's reverence for wood, Weber featured exotic, highly figured species such as padauk and zebrawood in his first boxes.

Gradually, Weber's boxes began to change as he realized that the pronounced grain patterns distracted from his designs. Sharp edges replaced the soft lines on his earlier work, and he began to experiment with ebony paired with holly or other

light-colored woods. Always a fan of old black-and-white movies, he sees something of that aesthetic reflected in his boxes. They also suggest Art Deco furniture.

The early years were difficult. A turning point came in 1983 when he was accepted into the American Craft Council Fair at Rhinebeck, New York. Things did not start out well when his van broke down en route, and he had to go into debt to get it fixed. But the show was a success, and he became a regular at six or seven craft shows a year, consistently winning honors. At the prestigious Smithsonian Craft Show in Washington, D.C., in 2008, his boxes were recognized as Best in Show.

Between shows, Weber spends a lot of time watching his wife Klara's constantly evolving work as a ceramic artist and developing new prototypes. Early in his career, Weber tried sketching his ideas, but he quickly found it worked best to settle on a basic shape and size and then begin

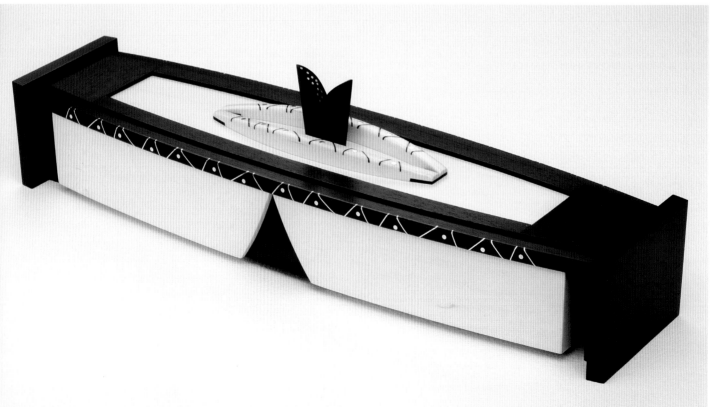

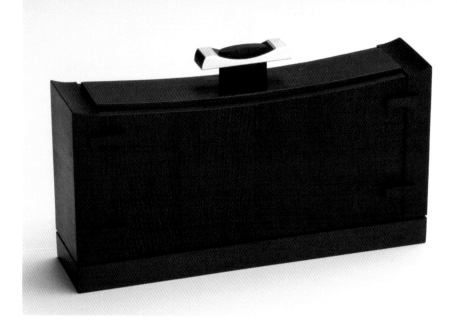

building, trial fitting parts until he was happy with the result. He would take each new prototype to shows and write orders. He keeps templates, extra parts, plans, and in many cases, a complete photographic record of how to assemble each design.

Some of his boxes—*Architecture 1* and *Structural Integrity*—acknowledge the influence of modern architecture with their names. The former sits on pylons like a Le Corbusier building and the latter has exposed ribs on the sides like girders supporting a skyscraper.

Only a few of his boxes have drawers. Most of his works have removable lids, even when they recall small sculptural objects. For example, *Linnet*, named for a

---

When he first began making boxes, Weber was not sure he could earn a living at it because he thought he worked too slowly.

---

species of finch, has folded ebony wings that enclose a Pacific yew body. *Black Tie* is formed by crossed pieces of ebony. Many of his rectangular boxes also suggest everyday objects. The shape of *Baby Grand* clearly references its name, and the spalted maple lid of *Thoroughbred* evokes a dirt racetrack. *Silver Bud* seems ready to burst into bloom, and *Design 99* takes the shape of a small fruit complete with a stem.

In 1984, he tired of the cold Maine winters and wanted to be closer to craft show venues. He and his wife found Effort, Pennsylvania, which is within a two-hour drive of Philadelphia and New York City. He works alone in a shop that is thirty feet

ABOVE

Coco, 2007. Ebony, brass; H. 2⅝" W. 4½" D. 1". Could *Coco* be a take-off on an exotic container by the well-known cosmetic baroness, Coco Channel? Weber's wife, Klara, thought so and gave it the name.

LEFT ABOVE

Midnight, 2007. Holly, ebony, silver; H. 3" W. 2¼" D. 2¼". As with most of Weber's work, *Midnight* is a study in shapes and their relationships. Two flat sides contrast with the two curved sides, and the handle echoes the curve.

LEFT BELOW

Primi Tivo, 2006. Ebony, black palm wood, silver; H. 1⅝" W. 1⅞" D. 3¾". The exposed silver pins could be eyes and the teardrop shape a mouth—primitive as in Primi, and Tivo as in the modern television recorder.

from his home, and Klara has her studio in the basement of the main house with plenty of window wells for natural light.

Oval Exploration evolved from a special box called *Freeport Farewell* that he made right before he left Freeport, Maine. And he had used the vertical slate motif on the sides of other boxes, including a recent series called *Set Sail*. The effect, which he calls

a fixed tambour, suggests the thin strips on a roll top desk. The slates on each end of *Oval Exploration,* however, are S-shaped, making this box among the most complex he has produced.

Oval Exploration took about eight days to make. First, he sawed the oval bottom out of plywood to provide a stable framework. Then he cut blocks for the slats and stuck

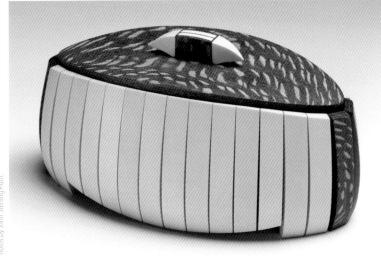

ABOVE

Kozma, 2008. Ebony, chakte viga; H. 1⅝" W. 5" D. 2¼". *Kozma* is an obvious reference to the early modernist architect, Lajos Kozma, whose work since the fall of the Iron Curtain has gained greater appreciation. Weber saw an exhibition of his work at a museum in Budapest. The lid is glued up from ten strips cut from the same block of wood as the sides.

LEFT

Set Sail, 2007. Holly, leopardwood, ebony; H. 2⅝" W. 6½" D. 3⅜". Although the shape of *Set Sail* suggests a ship, the title is more metaphorical.

them onto a backing so that he could shape them all at once using a small horizontal belt sander. The final step was to attach the horizontal sidepieces and assemble the lid. While he has used copper, brass, and mother-of-pearl inlay on other boxes, this one featured silver strips let into fine sawn slots to suggest stringing, and rods pressed into drilled holes to form tiny dots. Although he had used random patterns of dots in varying sizes before, the tiny dots in this example became part of a delicate banding reminiscent of early nineteenth century furniture inlay.

The most tedious stage of the project was the finish. He applied Thompson's water seal to the ebony and Krenov's recipe of shellac and alcohol to the holly. Keeping black ebony dust out of the pores of the white holly required repeated assembly, sanding, and disassembly until the final product was silky smooth. The wood seems almost as soft as the suede that covers the box bottom.

When he first began making boxes, Weber was not sure he could earn a living at it because he thought he worked too slowly. Some thirty years later, he is still a full-time box maker turning out more than 100 boxes a year. It is a labor of love—the love of creating something out of raw wood that people will cherish and hand down to their children.

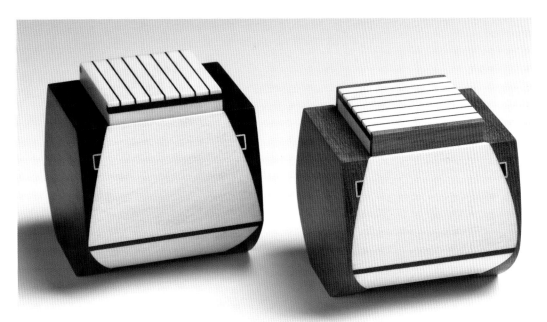

ABOVE TOP
Gateway, 2007. Ebony, chakte viga; H. 4⅝" W. 2⅞" D. 4". This little box conjures up a Japanese temple gate in the mind of the viewer.

ABOVE BOTTOM
The Eduardo Series, 2007. Holly, ebony, chakte viga, brass; H. 1⅞" W. 2" D. 2". Boxes in *The Eduardo Series* take on an anthropomorphic look with their square brass eyes and inlaid lines for mouths. Are they the Eduardo brothers?

HANS WEISSFLOG

Born: 1954, Honnersum, Germany

Meticulous Planning of Complex Designs

Hans Weissflog had no family exposure to craftsmanship and while growing up, encountered no role models to encourage him in the arts. After finishing secondary school, he enrolled in a two-year engineering program and became a technical draftsman for Bosch, a large German technology conglomerate and later for Blaupunkt, the car radio manufacturer. After his

About 15 years ago, the ball form evolved into a rocking ball when Weissflog applied solid laminations to half the sphere and either left the upper half open as a bowl, or added a hemisphere for a lid to make it into a box.

employer laid him off, a neighbor told him about a design program at a college in Hildesheim. He decided to return to school to pursue a degree in furniture and toy design. One of his professors was a well-known wood turner, so Weissflog decided to get a joint certificate in that field as well.

From the shop next to his boyhood home in the medieval German city of Hildesheim, he began to make craft items like baby rattles and children's toys before moving on to larger pieces such as lamps, furniture, and production work for other cabinetmakers. He also discovered boxes, which in the 1980s, few turners were making. He liked the diminutive form because by using small pieces of wood, he could afford to stock nearly 500 varieties from which to choose. His motto is "Klein und Fein"—"Small and Fine."

ABOVE

Hans Weissflog in his shop in Hildesheim, Germany.

OPPOSITE

Ball Boxes, 2008. Cocobolo (Dia. 4"); boxwood, African blackwood (Dia. 2½"); boxwood (Dia. 2"). Stand: Australian brown malle root.

A turning point in his career came during a turners' meeting at a Nuremberg museum where he saw some work done a century ago by a craftsman named Saueracre. The object was normally in storage but had been brought out for the conference. It was a flat piece of pierced work created on a special ornamental lathe. Struggling to develop his own style, Weissflog realized he could do the same thing with a standard lathe, and do it in the round.

Weissflog perfected the technique, and by the early 1990s, was a full-time artist. His work began to be recognized, and in 1994, he received the highest honor for a German craft artist, the Lower Saxony State Award. His signature *Ball Box* is his best-known piece, and he has done them from three-quarters of an inch up to ten inches in diameter. He turns the balls in solid wood or with two contrasting woods. He uses the lighter wood, often boxwood, on the inside and the darker, often African blackwood, on the outside. After gluing the spheres together, he turns the concentric circles in both woods. The resulting holes in the grooves between the circles form a lattice pattern. Several hours are required to clean up the holes after he finishes the turning.

About fifteen years ago, his ball form evolved into a rocking ball when he applied solid laminations to half the sphere and either left the upper half open as a bowl, or added a hemisphere for a lid to make it into a box. Because it is his most popular piece, he continues to make variations of the basic design. For him, the box has a spiritual quality with the solid part representing the earth and the light part, the heavens.

Beginning in the mid-1990s, after making boxes for a while, Weissflog scaled up the design to produce turned bowls. With a bigger surface to work with, he is able to decorate the bowls with varying configurations of circles. *Touching Rings*, for example, features a series of circles around the top of the bowl. Much to his surprise, a different lattice pattern in another bowl resembled a spider, hence *Spider Bowl* was born. The most difficult bowl he calls *Saturn* because its shape resembles the ringed planet, and as an added bonus, it too has the spider image in the bowl. A box version of this design features a free edge ring.

Creating eight or ten new models a year, Weissflog has done more than 100 different box designs. He enjoys visiting museums and observing the world around him, but most of his ideas are variations

Saturn Box, 1989. Boxwood burl; H. 3" W. 7" D. 5⁵⁄₁₆". *Saturn Box* was cut from a single piece of boxwood burl.

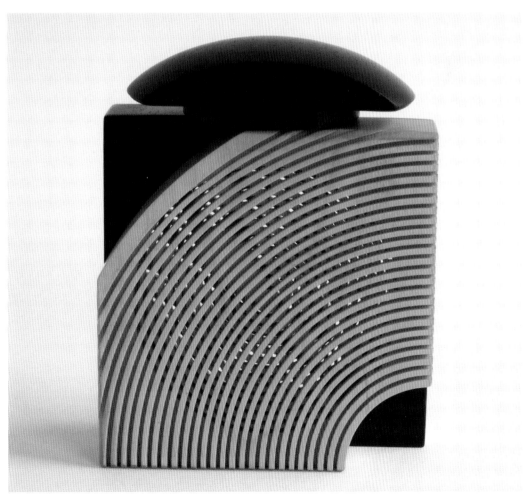

Ball Box, 1996. African blackwood, boxwood; Dia. 2". *Ball Box* is one of Weissflog's signature designs. He cuts the grooves from the inside to the middle of the wall and from the outside also to the middle of the wall. The holes appear where the grooves meet.

Quarter-Circle Box, 2002. Boxwood, ebony, African blackwood; H. 2⅞" W. 2⅜" D. 2⅜". To get the quarter-circle shape in *Quarter-Circle Box*, Weissflog puts four pieces of wood together and then turns a whole circle using only two of them.

on the distinctive style and techniques that he developed early in his career. In 2003, inspired by the attacks on New York's Twin Towers, he split two pieces of

Creating eight or ten new models a year, Weissflog has done more than 100 different box designs.

African blackwood with an ax and then inset two delicately turned disks into the slabs. Similar turned disks serve as lids on his cylindrical vessels. His *I Vessels* have a cylindrical base and a ball, like a dot, for the top. He is always experimenting with geometrical spheres, ovals, cubes, cones, and pyramids, as well as interesting amorphous forms like his *Big Drunken Box*. He has also combined two shapes, as in *Ball in a Square Lens*, *Captured Sphere*, and *Round Square Oval Box*.

Although he sometimes works with metal, plastic, and other materials, he prefers wood. Every species looks, smells, and behaves differently—just like people, he says. Still, he is always searching for new ideas, and several years ago, he turned a dome out of bone, mounted it on an ebony base, and called it *Little Ghost*. He has also inlaid bone disks and slices of the Malaysian areca palm into the lids of a series of wooden vessels. He also has made containers by hollowing out the fruit of the raphia palm found in Africa and South America.

After 2000, Weissflog began to give his work more presence, juxtaposing his controlled turning with raw surfaces by, for example, placing his ball boxes on pedestals of roughly carved wood. For *Ball Boxes*, he

ABOVE TOP

Round Square Oval Box, 2000. African blackwood, boxwood; H. 2" W. 2⁵⁄₁₆" D. 2⁵⁄₁₆". For *Round Square Oval Box*, Weissflog starts with a sphere, but from the top, the piece looks like a square and from the sides like ovals.

ABOVE BOTTOM

Saturn for D. Cortes, 1998. Boxwood; H. 1⅜" Dia. 3⅜". After Damaris Cortes criticized his work, Weissflog promised to name a box for the schoolgirl. The ring of *Saturn for D. Cortes* is loose, but it was all turned from one piece of wood.

features three different size boxes turned from three different hardwoods, all with little or no grain. Boxwood is especially precious, taking up to eighty years to reach a two-inch diameter. The balls sit in African blackwood cups that are stuck into a base made from the root of an Australian brown mallee shrub. As with most of his work, they are finished with two coats of nitrocellulose lacquer. One can imagine the ordered turnings representing life emerging from an amorphous primordial stew.

Many turners let the wood inspire their designs, and improvise as they shape the block on the lathe. Coming from a strong design background, Weissflog meticulously plans the fabrication of each piece. The designs are too complex to deviate from. Still, he always pushes the technical limits of the lathe and about one in three pieces shatters, forcing him to start all over. He fantasizes about making something with all the broken parts.

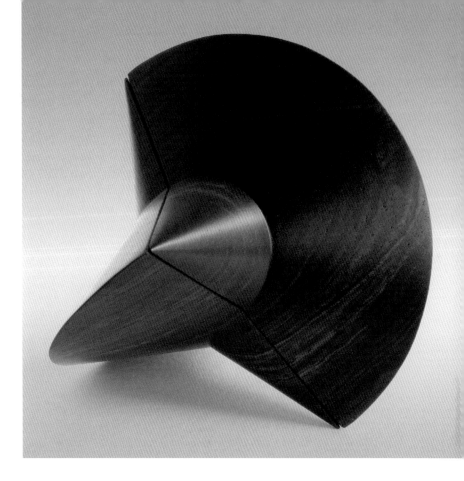

Proud of having revived and modernized the traditional craft of ornamental turning, Weissflog has had the satisfaction of passing on these techniques to the next generation. From the age of ten, his son, Jakob, has worked with him in the shop. Recently, Jakob completed a formal three-year apprenticeship program with his father and is now a certified turner. He helps with his father's business while developing his own body of work. Together, they are proving that what can be produced on the lathe has few limits.

ABOVE

Second Drunken Box, 1997. African blackwood; H. 2¹¹⁄₁₆" W. 3⅛" D. 2¹¹⁄₁₆". When *Second Drunken Box* rolls, it travels in two directions, like a "drunken box."

LEFT

Drunken Box, 1998. Ziricote; H. 2⅝" W. 3⅛" D. 2⅝". This is an alternate design for Weissflog's *Drunken Box*. The shape is turned, rotated ninety degrees, and turned again.

BIBLIOGRAPHY

Books

Bedford, John. *All Kinds of Boxes*. London: Cassell, 1969.

Clarke, Antigone and Joseph O'Kelly. *Antique Boxes: Tea Caddies and Society 1700-1880*. Atglen, PA: Schiffer Publishing, 2003.

Douglas, Diane; Michelle Holzapfel; Ursula Illse-Neuman, et. al. *Cabinets of Curiosities*. Philadelphia and Ashville, NC: The Wood Turning Center and The Furniture Society, 2003.

Edwards, Ralph. *The Shorter Dictionary of English Furniture*. New York: Country Life, 1964.

Fine Woodworking. Design Book Six. Newtown, CT: Taunton Press, 1992.

Gunter, Veronika Alice. (ed.). *400 Wood Boxes: The Fine Art of Containment & Concealment*. New York: Lark Books, 2004.

Hornung, Clarence P. *Treasury of American Design*. New York: Harry N. Abrams, Inc., 1950.

Ingham, Robert. *Cutting-edge Cabinetmaking*. Lewes, East Sussex, Great Britain: Guild of Master Craftsman Publications Ltd., 2007.

Ketchum, William C. Jr. *The Smithsonian Institution Illustrated Library of Antiques: Boxes*. New York: Cooper-Hewitt Museum, 1982.

Klamkin, Marian. *The Collector's Book of Boxes*. New York: Dodd, Mead, 1970.

Latham, Jean. *Collecting Miniature Antiques*. New York: Charles Scribner's Sons, 1972.

Little, Nina Fletcher. *Neat and Tidy, Boxes and Their Contents: Used in Early American Households*. New York: E. P. Dutton, 1980.

Lloyd, Peter. *Making Heirloom Boxes*. East Sussex, Great Britain: Guild of Master Craftsman Publications Ltd., 2006

_____ and Andrew Crawford. *Celebrating Boxes*. Fresno, CA: Linden Publishing, 2001.

Lydgate, Tony. *The Art of Making Elegant Wood Boxes: Award Winning Designs*. New York: Sterling Publishing Co., 1993

_____. *Award Winning Boxes: Design and Technique*. New York: Sterling Publishing Co., 1995.

_____. *The Art of Making Elegant Jewelry Boxes: Design and Techniques*. New York: Sterling Publishing Co., 1996.

_____. *The Art of Small Wood Boxes*. New York: Sterling Publishing Co., 1997.

_____. *Po Shun Leong Art Boxes*. New York: Sterling Publishing Co., 1998.

_____. *400 Wood Boxes: The Fine Art of Containment & Concealment*. New York: Lark Books, 2004.

Martin, Terry and Kevin Wallace. *New Masters of Woodturning*. East Petersburg, PA: Fox Chapel Publishing, 2008.

Menke, Donna LaChone. *The Ultimate Band Saw Box*. New York: Sterling Publishers, 2006.

Raffan, Richard. *Turning Boxes*. Newtown, CT: Taunton Press, 2002.

Reid, Bill and Robert Bringhurst. *The Raven Steals the Light*. Seattle: University of Washington Press, 1996.

Schleining, Lon. *Treasure Chests: The Legacy of Extraordinary Boxes*. Newtown, CT: Taunton Press, 2003.

Schiffer, Herbert F. and Peter B. Schiffer. *Miniature Antique Furniture*. Atglen, PA: Shiffer Publishing, Ltd., 1995.

Stowe, Doug. *Simply Beautiful Boxes*. Cincinnati: Popular Woodworking Books, 2000.

Wood Turning Center and Yale University Art Gallery. *Wood Turning in North America Since 1930*. Philadelphia, PA and New Haven, CT: Woodturning Center and Yale University Art Gallery, 2001.

Articles

Adamson, Glenn. "More Than Meets the Eye: Tom Loeser's Kinetic Furniture." *Woodwork* #72, December 2001, pp. 26-34.

Helferich, Omar Keith and Robert Sroufe. "The Jewel Box: A Life Cycle Case Study." Council of Logistics Management, 1996.

Heimerl, Cortney. "Tom Loeser: Talking Creative License." *American Craft*, Vol. 68 No. 6, December 2008/January 2009, pp. 064-071.

Martin, Terry. "Questioning the Limits: Canadian Woodworker Michael Hosaluk." *Woodwork* #70, August 2001, pp. 26-31.

_____. "Form, Function, and Fame: The Life Work of Richard Raffan." *Woodwork* #84, December 2003, pp. 22-28.

McFadden, Tom. "Where Engineering, Art, and Woodworking Meet: Michael Cullen." *Woodwork* #35, October 1995, pp. 30-38.

INDEX

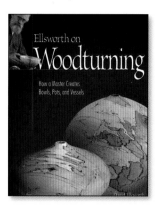
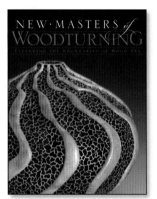
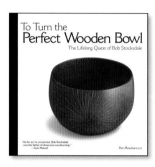
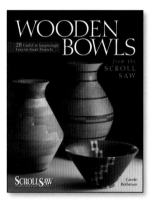
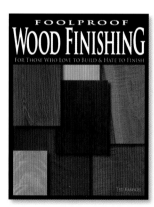